THE BUY
NOTHING,
GET EVERYTHING
PLAN

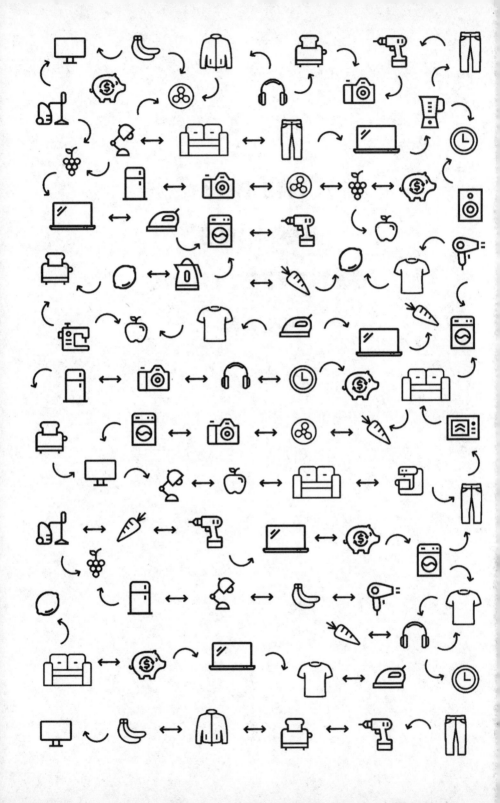

THE BUY NOTHING, GET EVERYTHING PLAN

Discover the Joy of Spending Less, Sharing More, and Living Generously

LIESL CLARK AND REBECCA ROCKEFELLER

Founders of the Buy Nothing Project

ATRIA BOOKS

New York • London • Toronto • Sydney • New Delhi

ATRIA
BOOKS

An Imprint of Simon & Schuster, Inc.
1230 Avenue of the Americas
New York, NY 10020

First Atria Books hardcover edition April 2020

ATRIA BOOKS and colophon are trademarks of Simon & Schuster, Inc.

For information about special discounts for bulk purchases, please contact Simon & Schuster Special Sales at 1-866-506-1949 or business@simonandschuster.com.

The Simon & Schuster Speakers Bureau can bring authors to your live event. For more information or to book an event, contact the Simon & Schuster Speakers Bureau at 1-866-248-3049 or visit our website at www.simonspeakers.com.

Interior design by Dana Sloan
Illustrations by Brooke Budner

Manufactured in the United States of America

1   3   5   7   9   10   8   6   4   2

Library of Congress Cataloging-in-Publication Data is available.

ISBN 978-1-9821-1379-7
ISBN 978-1-9821-1381-0 (ebook)

Dedicated to everyone who believes our money is best used on those things that build a healthy, joyful, and equitable world.

CONTENTS

THE BUY
NOTHING,
GET EVERYTHING
PLAN

INTRODUCTION

How We Came to Buy Less and Share More

Our story begins on a clear day in mid-December, a rare break between winter storms, on a wild beach not far from our Pacific Northwest community.

With the sun low in the sky, the light a pale wintry yellow, we walked along the beach with our children, watching four pairs of tiny bare feet trip through the sand. Although we wore winter coats, the temperature was just warm enough for the kids to leave their shoes in the car, a welcome freedom from wool socks and rain boots. The kids tiptoed barefoot across the up-shore jumble of enormous Douglas fir and western red cedar driftwood logs as if on a tightrope, playing an imaginary game of circus acrobatics. The water here was cold and deep, with a strong current and whitecaps between us and the hazy outline of Seattle's hills across the Salish Sea.

We—Liesl and Rebecca—had been close friends for a year, and our kids, ranging from ages four to seven, were often inseparable, spending their days exploring the outdoors. Their intrepid desire for exploration brought us to the wildest island shorelines we could find within after-school driving distance. Rebecca is a single mom with two daughters, Ava and Mira. She's a blogger and social media consultant who comes from a family of activists and politicians fighting for the environment, and Liesl is a documentary filmmaker whose lens captures cutting-edge science and exploration for *NOVA* and National Geographic. Many of her projects involve travel with her two children, Finn and Cleo, and her husband, Pete Athans. With our shared love of adventure and the natural world, excursions to wintry beaches of this kind were a regular thing for us, and this one was just like any other, until Finn got a splinter, the downside of barefoot beach walks. Liesl removed the offending barb before any tears could break the happy tone of the day, but we noticed something else clinging to the bottom of his feet . . . something that didn't belong. Tiny white balls of polystyrene foam and colorful minibits of plastic were lodged between his toes.

When we looked more closely at the sand beneath our feet, we found a couple of three-millimeter-wide plastic discs. (We later discovered these are called nurdles, and they are industrial feedstock for all plastic products.) It soon became clear that the discs made up an alarming percentage of the beach-scape that day. As the kids ran along the logs, yelling out with glee about their newfound game, refusing to touch the "plaastic saand" with their feet, we trained our gaze to look at what else was commingling with the sand, shells, driftwood, and seaweed around us. We found larger bits of plastic debris that were even more disturbing: syringes, a green army man that Finn was happy to add to his collection, coffee stirrers, PVC pipe, pens just like Cleo's from home, light switch covers, a Mylar helium birthday balloon like the one that Ava lost at a friend's party when it slipped free from her fingers the week before, cigarette lighters, a bright yellow baby toy just like one Mira remembered having, car bumpers, and tampon applicators—objects of our everyday lives, all made of plastic, all washed up on our shoreline.

Of course the plastic had been there all along; we just hadn't seen it until now. And once we saw it, we couldn't unsee it. All of these items, things we used and relied on every day, had made their way to our beaches and were hiding in plain sight, not so much overtaking the beach as actually becoming part of it.

We consider that day—two years before we launched the grass-roots and increasingly impactful Buy Nothing Project, which is now more than one million members strong with an astounding six thousand volunteers—to be the very beginning of our Buy Nothing journey. We stumbled upon a seemingly small island story that was really a big global problem, and it inspired us to bring about social change to combat the reality of excessive waste and plastics in our environment.

What does it mean to Buy Nothing? Put simply, it is a philosophy that holds that the key to a joyful life of meaning and abundance on a healthy planet is to pursue every possible alternative before buying anything one wants or needs. This is a philosophy we've been bringing to life through the Buy Nothing Project, a social collective of local gift economies—an alternative to the market economy that most of us rely on—in which neighbors share with neighbors, members "ask" for what they want instead of buying it, and members "give" away their gently used items instead of tossing them. What started as a revelation at the beach a few years ago has translated to neighbors in dozens of countries sharing their stuff and their talents locally, willingly staving off needless consumerism. But Buying Nothing means much more to us.

Buying Nothing is a shift in mind-set. It's a reminder of the truth in that old adage "One man's trash is another man's treasure"; that there's value in re-homing a once-loved, now unused item and giving it a new life, rather than condemning it to the attic or garage, or worse yet, the waste bin. In a sense, Buying Nothing is a shift back to the way of our grandparents, the way people lived in the age before one-click buying, when you called a neighbor if you ran out of sugar or were short on gas for the lawn mower.

Many of us have become unsatisfied, wanting much more than we need, forgetting the days when it was not only acceptable to wear your mother's or grandmother's wedding dress, but just how things were done. Our appetite for more is costing us a fortune, taking a toll on both our wallets and the environment. Discovering persistent plastics on our shoreline was a reality check for us, an urgent wake-up call to do something, anything, to start a conversation about our buying habits and, in turn, reverse the ever-growing trend of plastic pollution on Earth.

Some might say our dream of social change has come to fruition: we've launched a worldwide social movement of unrestrained giving and asking, receiving and sharing, all for free, with no strings attached. Buy Nothing has legs, and the positive side effects are addictive. In this new worldview—one based on a sharing-focused economy—everyone benefits, and anyone can take part: minimalists, maximalists, spendthrifts, community builders, and environmentalists alike. Our Buy Nothing experiment—featured in the *Washington Post*, Mother Nature Network, Grist, Yahoo News, the *New York Times*, Australia Broadcasting Company, NHK Japan, CBC News, *South China Morning Post*, and on NPR—is a true, modern gift economy model, a system in which goods and services are distributed as true gifts, freely given without any expectation of reward, never bartered, traded, or sold. Here, *real* sharing takes place, and no single person benefits above all. Each participant accrues social standing through their actions, and we each reap what we sow.

Maybe you've already embraced the Buy Nothing mind-set, or take part in one of the many trending "sharing economies," where companies like Uber, Lyft, Airbnb, and Vrbo have broken ground. People around the globe are sharing their homes and cars, building tiny homes, borrowing from municipal lending libraries, and otherwise finding ways to share resources they own. Much of this "sharing economy" still functions as part of the market economy, with money being exchanged for Uber rides and Airbnb vacation housing, for instance. Buy Nothing offers you a chance to extend this mind-set so that you are giving and receiving without spending any money at all.

This book is an invitation for you to join us, starting wherever you are now regarding the idea of Buying Nothing. We believe that we can all achieve greater personal happiness, more-resilient communities, and a healthier planet by creatively sharing what we have in abundance, and in this book we'll provide you with the steps to do it. You don't need anything other than your goodwill and a healthy human desire to connect with the people in your life. To inspire you, we've included many giving and sharing stories throughout this book. They're all true, with a few names and locations changed to protect privacy.

> We are all familiar with the three Rs of consumption: Reduce, Reuse, Recycle. For us, there was another important R that was missing: Refuse.

Let's stop buying, and try sharing more. This book is a blueprint for doing just that, helping you to consume fewer newly manufactured goods, and share the bounty that already surrounds us. We are all familiar with the three Rs of consumption: Reduce, Reuse, Recycle. For us, there was another important R that was missing: Refuse.

In July 2013, we initiated our first local gift economy in our hometown of Bainbridge Island, Washington, eight miles from Seattle's downtown ferry docks. We launched a Facebook group for our island population of twenty-three thousand and called it Buy Nothing Bainbridge. The group buzzed with activity as members quickly came to see that Buying Nothing was not just a plausible lifestyle, but a convenient means to meet the people who live down the street. By the end of the summer, we established eleven more Buy Nothing Project communities, and by New Year's we had launched seventy-nine local gift economies, reaching into five states, each with the same simple mission of encouraging members to share more with those who live immediately nearby. The idea was spreading quickly.

We were able to prove that anyone could Buy Nothing, asking for gifts before shopping and offering gifts instead of stockpiling or throwing out. Someone nearby probably has what you're looking for. Members shared every thing and service they could think of: bookshelves, baby joggers, house cleaning, bricks, laptops, bread makers, haircuts, and canoes. One of the first items shared was a spring to fix the inside of a toilet paper roll holder; someone posted it almost as a joke, but someone else needed it, and all of us realized in that interaction that the passing along of such a seemingly random but very useful item signaled that we could take care of one another. We each had things that other people needed or wanted, small things as well as big, and the joy in sharing these things was the same no matter the gift. We were hoping the Facebook groups would help decrease waste, which they did. But there was an unexpected benefit: neighbors got to know other neighbors, communities were strengthened, and new friendships were formed. Thanks to many acts of kindness, Buying Nothing caught on like a piece of good gossip.

We've found that there are three basic actions in a healthy gift economy that serve to strengthen the social fabric of any community: gives, asks, and expressions of gratitude. These three actions are the foundation of the Buy Nothing Project, and all of the local groups encourage members to "give" away an item that's no longer needed, "wish" for something they want or need, and post with "gratitude" for the old-new item that has a new home and purpose.

Here are just a few stories we've heard from various Buy Nothing groups: A woman starting chemotherapy in the winter asks for help with her garden and has fresh vegetables to eat, and new friends to eat them with, as she recovers her appetite in the spring. A single senior citizen asks for a wagon to pull her senior dog on their walks around the neighborhood and gets the perfect set of wheels. Baby clothes pass from family to family, a working coffee maker with a broken carafe is reunited with the perfectly good carafe of a broken coffee maker two blocks away. A child's school sock drive for the homeless results in thousands of single socks finding a new match. A young woman recovering from an eating disorder asks people to meet her in a local café each week to play Scrabble so that her body can rest after eating; responding neighbors become friends who celebrate her return to health over weekly games. Homes of middle-aged empty nesters filled with too much stuff empty out into homes of newlyweds just starting out. Brides find wedding dresses, and the elderly find playmates for a game of Parcheesi.

We have been delighted to see the creativity that members bring to the concept. Members have started seed libraries; lending libraries for dishes, glasses, and silverware for entertaining; and tool libraries. They gather to swap and share books, offer yarn for crocheting, offer their expertise leading mushroom and foraging expeditions, pass along clothing and recipes, teach cooking classes, gather for fruit-gleaning outings, organize free "shops" stocked with Halloween costumes and holiday gifts. They are not only curbing their purchases, but rediscovering the age-old value of sharing, as each gift has a story that goes with it, further connecting individuals and their histories with one another.

The secret? Making sure every gift is offered freely, with no expectation of something in return.

New groups are forming all the time. We're constantly responding to requests from strangers asking us to help them start their own local giving group. We provide them with training on how to be a compassionate leader of an online social group and how to grow and steward their local group. We also provide them with rules, images, and guidelines, all freely produced and given, as well as a support network of regional and global volunteers who are there to answer questions and help set up new groups. Buying Nothing works best in hyperlocal groups, so we recommend that groups form around neighbors within easy reach of one another; in rural areas, this looks different than in cities, but it makes a huge difference when groups match existing neighborhood access routes and have no more than one thousand active members (the sweetest spot is around five hundred).

Now, six years later, there are more than four thousand Buy

Nothing Project local gift economies on six continents, including all fifty US states, every state of Australia, and all provinces of Canada. We're proud to say that there are absolutely no paid staff. The heart and soul of the project is the thousands of volunteers who give their time and expertise to build and sustain the groups. The Buy Nothing Project is a global network of local gift economies run by another gift economy made up of real people, volunteers and members who believe there's value in sharing. People are Buying Nothing in droves.

While inspired by the Buy Nothing Project, this book goes beyond the social groups and offers new suggestions for how everyone can share—how to Buy Nothing—in any and all of our social settings, with or without the World Wide Web. We give practical advice on just what can be shared, what each of us can avoid buying, why these Buy Nothing actions will have a positive impact on the environment, and, perhaps most important, how to attract more like-minded givers and receivers through old-fashioned kindness and gratitude. We hope you'll treat this book like a workbook, using the margins and empty spaces to jot down your ideas and experiences. Once you've written in your copy and added ideas and thoughts, we hope you will pass the book on and encourage others to do the same. Your book can be a living document, much like our mothers' dog-eared cookbooks with their notes and scribbles in the margins mentioning special occasions when recipes were enjoyed, or reminders to add extra spices here and there. We would love for our book to be a gift of accumulated shared wisdom from all the book's readers.

Most of all, we want you to enjoy this self-paced experiential class in the art of Buying Nothing; bring your sense of humor and an acceptance of yourself. This is not an exercise in perfection, self-denial, or abnegation. There is no way to "fail" at Buying Nothing. It's a philosophy meant to be explored and brought to life in ever-changing ways that work for you, wherever you are in your life right now. Celebrate your successes, no matter how small they seem, and remember that our seven-step challenge is meant to improve your life. If one of our suggestions doesn't help, by all means set it aside. You might want to flip through the steps to see what's coming, or you may prefer the surprise of meeting each challenge as it comes. You can devote a day, a week, or longer to each step. Set your own speed, and tackle each step when you feel ready for it. There's no wrong way to approach this book and the action plan it maps out. We encourage you to chart your own course as you build your own Buy Nothing mind-set and habits. And, of course, we hope you'll share this book and what you learn from it widely.

Although we've both had very different life experiences, what we've each learned has led us to the same truth: being knit into a local web of sharing in which we each play a vital role is more fulfilling than the lonely hoarding of stuff for our own private use. We believe that the good life we seek is more likely to lie in the abundance of sharing, that active generosity brings a sense of purpose to our lives, and that the most solid safety we have in times of want comes from being rooted in a giving culture, in which we are comfortable giving freely and receiving directly from one another, without any shaming or strings attached.

> **Buying everything disconnects us from one another; Buying Nothing plugs us in.**

You might say we're shining a bright light on an alternative way of living, where buying is seen as a last option in the pantheon of choices we can make each day in our communities. Buying everything disconnects us from one another; Buying Nothing plugs us in. We'd like to bring about social change. To do this, we're challenging you to stop buying. It doesn't have to be painful, or deprive you of what you love. We believe that if you try the steps outlined in this book, you'll come to see that Buying Nothing can get you just about, well, everything.

WHY WE SHOULD BUY NOTHING

So, how did we go from a child's splinter on the beach to launching a global experiment about giving more? It all comes back to plastics, of course.

After that day at the beach, we became women on a mission. With our kids in tow, we circumnavigated Bainbridge, the little island in Puget Sound we call home, to learn more about the continuous influx of plastics. We recovered carloads worth of plastic waste that washed up on the shores with each high tide. We picked up plastic chunks as large as a VW Bug, bits the size of a microfiber, and everything in between.

We became obsessed with the etiology of beach plastics and spent three years cleaning up local shorelines, cataloging every kind of household plastic, from buckets, toothbrushes, straws, bubble wrap, zip-top bags, packing peanuts, and Styrofoam meat trays, to the ever-present plastic water bottle and cap. We became citizen scientists, striving to answer the critical question: *Where did the plastics polluting our sands and waters come from?*

The Plastic Age

Of course, it came from all of us—our homes, our backyards, our cars, parking lots, workplaces, schools, and restaurants. If it was made of plastic and any of us on Bainbridge had purchased it, there was a high likelihood we'd see it wash up on our island one day. That summer, we studied our small island as a microcosm of the world at large. Through our observations, we were able to confirm that plastic is forever. It doesn't biodegrade. It simply breaks down into progressively smaller pieces, so small that in some parts of our oceans, microplastics, defined by the National Oceanic and Atmospheric Administration as minute pieces of plastic that are "less than five millimeters in length (or about the size of a sesame seed),"[1] outnumber zooplankton, the minuscule creatures in the sea that are the main source of food for many sea animals, by six to one.[2] There are two breakdown processes that deserve attention. The first is the breaking down of large items into microplastics. This matters because the smaller the piece, the more likely it is to be ingested by marine life and enter the food chain. We have seen firsthand that plastics that enter the environment as whole items can become microplastics rather quickly when they meet with forces such as vehicles, sunlight, and waves. A pen dropped from a pocket and then run over by a car on its way to the nearest body of water goes from whole to small shards with one pass under a tire. In a matter of weeks, a plastic shopping bag caught by the wind can turn to shreds resembling seaweed when weakened by sunlight and tree branches, or a balloon can deflate and begin to tear apart into a tentacled blob resembling a jellyfish. Once plastics are caught up in the same natural forces that smooth beach rocks and polish shells, they begin to take on organic shapes that fool the human eye and those of marine life, too. Larger, more intact pieces of plastic waste may not fool a hungry animal, and they're too big to be sucked up by a filter feeder, but it doesn't take long at all for many plastic items to lose their original shape and begin to break into microplastics that are more likely to be ingested by marine life. It is estimated that the entire photodegradation process of microplastic takes 450 years for a plastic bottle and at least 600 years for a monofilament fishing line.[3] Plastics are the largest contributor to marine debris today, comprising 60 to 80 percent of the man-made trash in oceans worldwide, and 90 percent of all floating particles are plastic.[4]

We embarked on a months-long research project, scouring every shoreline we could access, and walked every beach and watershed around us. Each heavy rainfall unearthed more straws, bread tags, and cigarette lighters: they float downstream into estuaries and out to sea. We documented, firsthand, with video and photos, all of the debris. We created spreadsheets listing items, locations, and dates to geo-reference the accumulating plastics in our immediate environment, from the wilderness to urban landscapes. We pored over maps and data.

We came to realize that plastics move from the original consumer, wherever they are, to watersheds and waterways, eventually spilling into the sea. Most plastics are carried to our waters via urban runoff through storm drains, watersheds, and sewage. With nearly nine million tons of plastics per year entering our seas, it is estimated that by 2050 there will be more plastic, pound for pound, than fish in our oceans.[5]

No beach on our planet is free from plastic, few rivers can boast an absence of it, and our land itself is bubbling up with plastic in the least expected places. Our so-called organic gardens are loaded with plastics—organic compost sold by compost facilities is often laden with microplastics like threads of torn-up plastic bags. In short, we have a very serious plastic problem.

> **Plastics floating in the ocean act as an attractant for persistent organic pollutants such as DDT and PCBs, adsorbing these toxic chemicals, which then transfer to living organisms and increase in toxicity as they bioaccumulate in their journey to the top of each food chain.**

One of the world's only research laboratories studying microplastics in the environment is at the Center for Urban Waters in Tacoma, only sixty miles away from Bainbridge. At a conference on microplastics, the institute's science director, Dr. Joel Baker, spelled out what researchers know so far:[6]

- **Fact #1:** Other than the small bits of plastic that have broken down over time into microplastics, including microfibers from our clothing, another commonly recognized major source of microplastics originates from personal and cosmetic products employing microbeads and glitter in makeup, exfoliants, body wash, toothpaste, and facial scrubs.[7] Only recently have scientists begun to realize that microplastics this small may present a long-term threat for marine food chains that mistake the minuscule plastics for food. Plastic litter affects at least 800 species worldwide, including half of all sea turtles and 60 percent of our seabird species,[8] and it kills 100,000 marine mammals each year.[9]
- **Fact #2:** Plastics floating in the ocean act as an attractant

for persistent organic pollutants such as DDT and PCBs, adsorbing these toxic chemicals, which then transfer to living organisms and increase in toxicity as they bioaccumulate in their journey to the top of each food chain.[10] According to Merriam-Webster, adsorption is "the adhesion in an extremely thin layer of molecules (as of gases, solutes, or liquids) to the surfaces of solid bodies or liquids with which they are in contact." Not only are plastics floating everywhere in the ocean, but they act as a magnet for icky pollutants, the chemicals adhering to and surrounding the plastics themselves. Worse yet, scientists are now able to prove that plastics, and the chemicals they adsorb, can be found in the stomachs of seabirds as well as the fish and shellfish we consume.[11]

As a society, we are in the throes of what some scientists call the Plastic Age; we've made as much plastic in the past thirteen years as we have in the past century. How much plastic are we talking about? An article in the *Telegraph* summarized a study by researchers at the University of Georgia and University of California this way: "Plastic weighing the equivalent of one billion elephants has been created since the 1950s . . . by 2015 humans had generated 8.3 billion tons of plastics and 6.3 billion tons had become waste. Only 9 percent of the waste plastic was recycled, 12 percent was incinerated and 79 percent had accumulated in landfill or the natural environment. If current trends continue, roughly 12 billion tons of plastic waste will be in landfills or polluting oceans by 2050."

An infographic in the same article offers other comparisons for us to visualize. If you have trouble picturing one billion elephants, try 25,000 Empire State Buildings, 822,000 Eiffel Towers, or 80 million blue whales. Each of these represents the weight of all the plastic produced by humans as of 2015, and the majority of that has become waste.[12]

A Clean Solution

Now that we were painfully aware of how much toxic plastic washed up on our own beaches, we made it our mission to raise awareness in our community. We went into classrooms and conducted waste audits, helping the students to see how they could reduce their own waste footprint at school and at home. They joined us on our beach cleanups, and challenged us, at first believing that these beaches they'd grown up on had no plastics on them. One student gathered up a ball of seaweed and spread it over his hand, almost dropping it when he realized it was a green-algae covered bag. Others were surprised to see that the three-foot-long black tubes weren't bull kelp. They were PVC pipe, and why was that on the beach? The oval black mussel-shell-shaped items were plastic fireworks capsules, remnants from the Fourth of July. Small white round skeletal shapes were not fish vertebrae but cigarette filters. Tall strands of seagrass were actually straws and the funnels of ink pens. Plastic bottle caps mimicked clamshells, and woven through the streaming strands of seaweed along the wrack line were ribbons from helium balloons set free during local celebrations and memorials. This educational outreach with the schools was cathartic for us, but we knew we needed to do more than we were doing on a local level and expand our horizons.

We had to do something to either find answers or be a part of the solution, so we set out to tackle the problem at its root cause:

consumption. The best solution was to refuse to buy plastics in the first place. We started with ourselves, and within a matter of months we nearly aced the zero-waste-shopping thing.

But the pollution of our land and waters is only one part of the plastics problem. Greenhouse gas emissions are another. A study of household consumption in forty-three countries, published in 2016 in the *Journal of Industrial Ecology*, revealed that consumers are responsible for more than 60 percent of Earth's greenhouse gas emissions. Even more surprising is the fact that four-fifths of the environmental impacts that can be attributed to consumers are not "direct impacts," like the fuel we burn when we drive our cars or heat our homes, but are "secondary impacts," the environmental effects of producing the goods we buy.[13]

We found the answer we were looking for: if we consume less, we can greatly affect our overall individual carbon footprint. The average North American produced 16.4 metric tons of carbon dioxide in 2014.[14] This is equivalent to the carbon dioxide emissions from burning 17,929 pounds of coal per person.[15] Whenever we find an alternative to buying a brand-new item, we reduce our impact upon the environment in two ways: less carbon dioxide is emitted in the production and transportation of the item to market, and one less item is eventually headed to our landfills or into our watersheds and oceans. The world's leading climate scientists have warned we have less than a dozen years for global warming to be kept to a maximum of 1.5 degrees Celsius (approximately 2.7 degrees Fahrenheit).[16] Beyond that point, by even half a degree, we will significantly worsen the risks of drought, floods, and extreme weather events like heat, hurricanes, and wildfires, bringing with them poverty for hundreds of millions of people.

This sounds dire, we know, but there's an easy solution to

much of the problem: consuming less is perhaps the most powerful individual step we can all take to help with this environmental crisis. There must be a benefit of decreasing consumption and embracing a new life philosophy that's more gift- and less purchase-oriented.

The Psychology of Consumerism

Of course, Buying Nothing, at least at first, isn't easy—sometimes it seems as if we humans are hardwired to buy. But why?

We've spent a lot of time talking to Buy Nothing Project members and exploring our communal obsession with _stuff_. Why is it so hard to part with objects, even ones we rarely use or don't need anymore? Why are we constantly compelled to acquire more and more things, beyond what any one person needs? What hidden forces are driving our collective desire for stuff?

Based on close observation of people and their stuff in Buy Nothing groups, we formed some theories to answer these questions. Yes, we are targeted by more-personalized advertising than ever before, and yes, social media is a constantly refreshed stream of photos that show artfully arranged belongings and the seemingly perfect lives that go with them, and surely these forces inspire some of our consumption. But we saw something deeper happening. People seem to view their stuff as tangible aspects of their identity, and as proof of their worth, value, and existence and importance in the universe. It's as if there is an "I have stuff, therefore I am" logic at work. It turns out there are many psychologists conducting research into our relationships with our stuff, and their findings line up with our observations.

Research on this subject dating back as far as 1932 explains the deeply rooted human connections to stuff that we see every day in each gift economy we've helped set up: well before we are susceptible to marketing, before the age of two, we show strong feelings of ownership over stuff, and our relationship with our belongings goes from toddler fights over toys, to deep connections with a beloved stuffed animal, to finding solace in our stuff while we are teens struggling with feelings of low self-worth, to the conscious construction of our identities through our stuff. During our adult years, our possessions gain importance as they further express how we view ourselves, and also serve to hold memories of important life events, rites of passage, and beloved people. As we grow older still, our stuff keeps us company, standing in for days long past and people lost. At each stage of life from adolescence on, low self-esteem, lack of social connection, and feelings of powerlessness are tied to an increased focus on the importance of belongings. This connection between our sense of self and our things seems to be wired into us: scans of our brains show that the region used to think about our self-identity also lights up when we think about objects we own.[17]

Our complex and psychologically important relationship with our belongings, and the ease of obtaining more of them, means our homes are literally overrun with stuff, which isn't healthy for the environment or for us.

Drowning in Stuff

It's so easy to accumulate stuff, we're finding we have no room in our homes to store it anymore. More Americans each year are opting to rent storage space for their excess stuff. Today, there are at least forty-five thousand self-storage facilities in the US, and 9.4

percent of Americans rent them. Twenty years ago, there were half that number.[18]

From 2001 to 2005, a team of UCLA archaeologists from the Center on the Everyday Lives of Families conducted the first study of its kind with thirty-two dual-income middle-class families in the Los Angeles area designed to study their "material culture," the stuff of our everyday lives.[19] The archaeologists, Jeanne E. Arnold, Anthony P. Graesch, Enzo Ragazzini, and Elinor Ochs, conducted video tours of the family homes, led by each member of the households older than age seven. They systematically inventoried the objects in each room, mapping them, photographing them, and counting them—a monumental task. They documented every visible object in the thirty-two houses and took more than twenty thousand photos.

In one of the homes, they found 2,260 possessions in just three rooms (two bedrooms and the living room), not including "untold numbers of items tucked into dresser drawers, boxes and cabinets or items positioned behind other items." A good percentage of the objects of desire in our homes are plastic, contributing greatly to the study's finding that the average American home is filled with more than 300,000 items. Interestingly, they found a correlation between the number of magnets on refrigerators and the amount of stuff in the household.

> **The average American home is filled with more than 300,000 items.**

As the lead author, Jeanne E. Arnold, explained in an interview about the study, "Contemporary US households have more possessions per household than any society in global history. And hyper-consumerism is evident in many spaces, like garages, corners of home offices, and even sometimes in the corners of living rooms and bedrooms, and the kitchen, and the top of the dining room table, the shower stalls. We find lots of stuff, piles of stuff, and it's clearly, in some of these households, creating some significant stress for the families, particularly the mothers."[20]

They looked at cortisol levels, a stress hormone produced by our adrenal glands, in the women in the study and found them to be very high. They also noted that while we have many rituals and processes for accumulating objects, we have few for unloading or getting rid of them. We have an advertising industry geared toward encouraging us to purchase things. And since we've found cheaper and more efficient ways to produce more stuff, there is plenty available for purchase. This, coupled with the fact that buying has never been easier, means that we're accumulating more stuff than ever before.

The Unexpected Joy of Buying Nothing

Of course ease of buying and other factors have contributed to our overabundance of things, but we think there's something more primal than the desire for social status and wealth, something much more ancient than marketing campaigns behind our obsession with things. We think it comes down to the need to share the stories our things help us tell.

While we were educating ourselves about the history of plastic and plastic goods, we came across the Object Ethnography Project, founded by Max Liboiron, then a student at New York University. This project examines the relationships between people, their objects, and their histories. Ordinary people sent in objects they wanted to donate along with their story about the object. Other people could request a donated object in exchange for offering up a new story about it.[21]

Learning about this project was a lightbulb moment for us. Shared stories become unifying cornerstones in a community. They knit people together, help form group identities, and help us see ourselves as important within our groups. As we have become less connected with one another, our things have become the holders of our stories, reminding us that we matter. This is the crux of where we are as a society: our increasing isolation has led us to accumulate more than we can manage, and makes it harder to let go. As mothers, citizen scientists, and creators of the Buy Nothing Project movement, we believe connecting and sharing stuff *and* stories with those around us makes the letting-go process more meaningful and ties us to a collective consciousness that has been with us from the earliest human days. Historically, people have survived difficult times by cooperating to share resources. The impulse to help one another through gifts and sharing is still present and visible today, both in indigenous giving cultures that have withstood the challenges of colonization and capitalism and in the way people of all cultures spring to action during natural disasters such as droughts, hurricanes, and landslides. As climate change brings us more environmental change, our natural inclination to care for one another will have many new outlets for expression.

We also have a fundamental belief that living the good life is achieved through both extrinsic and intrinsic goals. We dream of living in abundance, an extrinsic goal we hope each of us can attain. But we also believe in the greater intrinsic goal of personal growth, connecting with others, feeling safe and valued, and building community. These goals are not mutually exclusive. In fact, we can satisfy both through Buying Nothing. When we give, receive, and share with one another, we can accumulate that which we desire (extrinsic) even as we strengthen our ties to the local community (intrinsic).

We've seen time and again in Buy Nothing groups that while members are often initially happy satisfying their extrinsic values, they keep participating because of the intrinsic benefits. In fact, these intrinsic benefits might be even more valuable than the extrinsic goal of accumulating more *stuff*. Numerous studies have found that when people prioritize intrinsic goals over extrinsic ones, higher levels of vitality and satisfaction are found, along with lower levels of depression and anxiety.[22]

As an added bonus, those who organize their lives around their intrinsic values like connectedness and deeper self-awareness, tend to treat others with kindness and live more ecologically sustainable lifestyles. In this way, Buying Nothing is a win-win.

Members aren't just surprised at the joy that comes from new connections and being part of a social movement. Some people come face-to-face with hidden behaviors and habits that are stubborn and hard to break, like shopaholic-ism, Depression-era-style hoarding, or the ego-challenging discomfort of asking for what we want. In many ways, these issues get to the heart of the Buy Nothing movement: understanding the hidden needs driving our consumerism and accumulation of things helps us identify and meet our deeper needs, the intangibles such as identity, connections, and self-worth that we need more than new stuff. Breaking a habit or even an addiction to buying stuff could be one of the hardest things you try to do, and for some it's the most challenging part of Buying Nothing. But just because you're not purchasing items doesn't mean you have to give up on getting things; gift economies are filled with stuff that neighbors are giving away. The benefit of sharing more is that we're consuming less collectively, and therefore saving money, reducing clutter, preventing plastics from polluting our oceans, and reducing greenhouse gases, all at once.

The Buy Nothing, Get Everything Plan gives us a window into all of these aspects of ourselves, and you're bound to learn some unexpected lessons and gain new insights into yourself as you work through the steps in this book. Sometimes these lessons may make us uncomfortable as we come face-to-face with our hidden needs or unhealthy habits, or learn to lean into the vulnerability of asking for what we need. But it's worth it. Not only will you come away feeling healthier and lighter thanks to your new Buy Nothing lifestyle—as will your bank account!—but your community will be stronger, having practiced the lost arts of giving, sharing, and receiving more. Sharing begets self-knowledge and also resilience.

But we're getting ahead of ourselves here. The first step is to show you how to buy less, as mindfully as possible. In doing so we explore our own emotional relationship with stuff and the reasons why we are consuming, and hence wasting, things now more than ever in history. We invite you to join us on this Buy Nothing journey, starting with the seven-step challenge.

AN INVITATION TO BUY NOTHING

Try Our 7-Step Buy Nothing Challenge

Here's your official invitation to join us in this experiment, to see if we can each find alternatives to buying what we want and to think twice before tossing something. Throughout this book, we'll provide you with a blueprint for changing your mind-set and behavior. Whether you're running out to the store to get something you think you need for your house, ordering a gift for a friend's birthday, or trying to make sense of the chaos in your closets, this book can help you curb your reliance on retail, limit your waste, and find creative ways to meet your needs and wants without spending money.

Not only will you save money, make new friends, receive things you want, and get rid of unwanted junk (without filling landfills!), you may be surprised to discover the serendipitous lessons and joy that come from reconnecting with the real world and people around you. This blueprint truly is for everyone, no matter where you live or your economic circumstances; gift economies work for all of us because we all have access to the same innate generous human nature.

Try to Buy No Thing, Buy Nothing, for as long as you can. Start small, with one week, perhaps. You may surprise yourself. Some people have succeeded in going for a year without even planning it, letting their new mind-set sustain them month after month. Every nillionaire (a pioneer who has bought nothing for months or years) we've met has these things in common: they're resourceful, deeply connected to others, and have a healthy perspective on the trappings of commercialism. We hear them talk about the abundance they live in, rather than the deprivations they have felt by not buying. Because we aren't buying the things we acquire and are relying more on the community to support us, Buying Nothing brings special meaning to how we shape our interdependence with family, friends, and neighbors.

For best results, add friends: Invite others to work through this book with you, checking in via phone or email or over a weekly cup of coffee. We also invite you to join us in the discussion forum at buynothinggeteverything.com so you have company along the way. It's invaluable to have others tackling these seven steps with you, for inspiration and venting alike, ranting and raving. You don't need to be in the same city, all that matters is following the same steps, wherever you are.

If you'd rather go it alone, we suggest keeping a journal to track your progress so you can take note of your triumphs and the memories, feelings, ideas, and stories that come from the challenge. We include an invitation at the end of each Buy Nothing step: *We Invite You to . . .* These are our suggestions for concrete behavioral actions you can try as part of this challenge. Checking in with yourself, your friends, and our online discussion forum at each step will help these changes take root and grow in your life and around the world.

If you want to get even more from these seven steps, we encourage you to see the "Rethink Your Trash" section on page 233, which is filled with ways to decrease your waste by rethinking what you throw away and coming up with new ways to toss less and repurpose more.

The Rules

The rules are simple: Buy Nothing, *buy no thing*, for as long as you can, other than the allowed expenses we list below. In each step, we provide exercises to get you started and help shift your behavior. The exercises are an integral part of the challenge, crafted to optimize your Buy Nothing experience and help you make long-lasting changes to your buying habits. The seven steps, briefly outlined, are as follows, and this book will guide readers through each step in greater detail, providing all of the support, encouragement, and information you need to be successful:

Step 1: Give—We explore the many forms of giving and suggest ways for you to start your own journey of generosity.

Step 2: Ask—When all gifts have equal value and are not monetized, the playing field is leveled and we're on equal footing. Asking for what you want is essential to the health of the gift economy.

Step 3: Reuse & Refuse—We offer tricks and tips to Refuse buying everyday things in the first place.

Step 4: Reflect—We investigate the hidden needs behind your desire to buy more, helping you stop the knee-jerk reaction to buy and come up with alternative ways to source what you need.

Step 5: Make & Fix—Celebrate the maker in you, reduce your waste footprint, and feel empowered to fix just about anything before buying new.

Step 6: Share, Lend & Borrow—We help you brainstorm creative ideas on how to share, lend, and borrow more.

Step 7: Gratitude—The essential superglue that binds us all together and begets more giving is openly expressing our thanks to those who have shared with us.

Exceptions

We know what you're thinking: But how will I eat? How will I live? Not to worry. Here's the list of expenses that are allowed, or even encouraged, during your Buy Nothing challenge:

1. Meals (food, especially locally grown, including eating out)
2. Regular household bills (heating, water, electricity, rent/mortgage)
3. Travel (includes bus/train fare, fuel, car insurance, car repair)
4. Prescriptions and personal care items (including toiletries for you, your dependents, and your pets)
5. Education (includes materials of all kinds, school bills, school events, other educational- or work-related events)
6. Stamps and shipping costs (not including shipping supplies)
7. Charitable/political contributions
8. Experiences and events (museum tickets, concerts, swimming at the pool with the kids, going to the zoo, visiting your state or national park, campsite fees, etc.)
9. Arts, culture, and the humanities (expenses that support

artists, scholars, and authors such as art, books, poetry, and musical recordings)

The purpose of this challenge is twofold: We're encouraging you to connect with your social network—or create new ones— to ask for what you need and to unload that which you no longer want to keep. But we're also helping you rethink your "wants." Do you really need those new plastic coat hangers if there are people nearby who would love to off-load theirs instead of throwing them away? Or do you have to buy that tent if a coworker has one she'd love to loan you? Does your bicycle need replacing or does it just need a good tune-up? Perhaps you can live without that "must-have" or you can find creative ways to get it, or repair it, without opening your wallet. Making things, fixing them, asking others for help, to borrow from, or to give to you are all part of taking an active role in your community. We are wired to connect with one another. And for most of our existence as a species we have relied on cooperative networks of sharing and giving for our survival. For all of the reasons we've shared so far, we could argue that embracing a Buy Nothing mentality is necessary for our survival now, too, using our modern connection methods and our abundance of stuff.

STEP 1: GIVE

The first step toward embracing a Buy Nothing mentality is to give. In some ways giving is a simple and natural act, something that's in our very nature to do, exemplified by the way a mother gives of herself to carry, birth, and nourish her baby. No matter the particulars of our entrance into the world or the genders and titles of our primary caregivers, none of us would be here today if it weren't for the vital gift of care we received when we were newborns unable to meet our own needs. But after this most vulnerable time in our lives, things become much more complicated, especially in a capitalist society. Once we move beyond our toddler years, we're encouraged to be independent and self-reliant, exploring our surroundings and collecting resources to care for ourselves. Later, in adolescence and adulthood, we discover the rewards of selling our labor and our things instead of giving, and we don't always recognize the full value of our talents, objects, or experiences without attaching monetary value to them. This chapter asks you to experiment with giving, to see offering gifts to others as the first step in creating a network of mutual dependence with those around you. We offer various ways you can give to individuals in your life and to the community at large.

To explore why giving is key, we need to look to the past. One of our formative lessons in, and inspirations for, Buying Nothing came from the wisdom of a people we've never known, whose stories were never told or even documented until recently.

Himalayan Teachings

Every summer for the past decade, Liesl's family has traveled to the Nepal-Tibet border to explore ancient caves nestled in the Himalayas at thirteen thousand feet. The caves have been there since before anyone can remember, and yet no one has been able to access them. Liesl's husband, Pete Athans, is a Himalayan climber and has the technical skill to get into these high cliff caves. With the support of the National Science Foundation, the couple and a multidisciplinary team of scientists, led by Dr. Mark Aldenderfer, professor of archaeology at the University of California, Merced, are among the first humans to enter these caves in hundreds, if not thousands, of years. For Liesl and her family, it's the privilege of a lifetime, one granted thanks to a multiyear permit with the government of Nepal and permission from the local communities. Together with some of the world's great scholars on Himalayan prehistory as well as geneticists and archaeologists, Liesl and her husband venture to these man-made caves to document and inventory their contents, recovering bones for ancient DNA testing to learn more about who the early people were and how they came to live and die in the most inhospitable place on Earth.

In one set of caves in the Upper Mustang region of Nepal, the team has uncovered a hidden network of burial chambers from a community that lived 1,450 years ago.[1] This community eked out a living at high altitude for more than 400 years, and are among the first people to have permanently settled one of the toughest places humans can survive on Earth. Their bones tell us they lived relatively healthy lives despite the harsh conditions, a testimony to cultural survival against all odds. From their burial artifacts and indeed the ceremonial manner in which they were interred, it is evident they relied on and cared for one another and traded extensively with people from the far east for silk and from the west and south for metals and beads.

It's thought that their lifestyle was not dissimilar to the Nepalese people who live half a mile away in a small village called Samdzong, only reachable if you walk for four hours from the nearest "road," over a high pass and through a canyon, to the idyllic valley they call home. The people of Samdzong have taught us a valuable lesson about the bonds of giving, asking, and expressing gratitude that can keep a community alive and thriving for generations. Today's villagers continue to trade for much of what they need, utilizing their prize cash crop: goats. They also communally care for one another and are mindful of what the land can sustain. They have a nearly egalitarian, mostly cash-free economy that connects families in a web of interdependence. It is, in other words, a modern-day, fully functioning gift economy.

In many ways, this small community inspired us to bring the idea of a gift economy to our hometown in the form of the Buy Nothing movement. In stark contrast to our Western capitalist society, a true gift economy functions if everyone can play the role of both giver and receiver, as Liesl discovered firsthand.

A NOTE FROM LIESL

Eight tents lined the edge of an unplanted field in the Nepalese village of Samdzong at fourteen thousand feet—yellow nylon pods sticking out like sore thumbs in the arid brown landscape known as the rain shadow of the Himalayas. My husband, two children, and I hauled five duffel bags' worth of warm clothing out of our four-person tent. The intention was to give the clothes to families there in thanks for yet another field season collaborating together on the cave excavations. We started making discrete piles of children's clothing, men's jackets and boots, women's sweaters, sunglasses, and more as the entire village gathered to look on and help with the distribution.

The headwoman, the *mukhia*, a fortysomething mother, walked over to me, leaned in, and politely advised (in Nepali), "You should divide the clothing equally into seventeen piles for the seventeen village households, each pile given equal amounts of adult and children's clothes." Slowly, in English, because my Nepali isn't all that understandable, I responded, "Yes, but I know that one household has only the sixty-eight-year-old woman in it." I bent over to remove the baby clothes from the pile for the sixty-eight-year-old woman, to make room for more adult clothing. I thought perhaps the mukhia had not fully understood my English, or my reasoning, so I was probably overgesturing, as foreigners tend to do. My kids looked on, embarrassed.

The mukhia had clearly understood. "The children's clothing in the old woman's pile," she explained with grace, laughing a bit at my ignorance, "ensures this village elder will have something to give. The health of our local village is dependent upon each family receiving the same gifts, so they can, in turn, be both giver and receiver."

The village's gift economy requires that each household is given the same amount of social capital, or equal ability to regift the items they didn't need to families that needed them. Social capital can be defined as the productive social relationships in any community that make up the true web of mutual bonds. Because of this, tiny baby socks are as useful to the sixty-eight-year-old woman as a pair of snow boots her size. When the time is right, she'll give the socks to a family with a new baby and strengthen her ties to that family. A fifty-year-old mother of adult children was thrilled to receive a kaleidoscope so she could play more readily with the village kids. A young man with small feet happily received large-size men's hiking boots so he could regift them to the right person.

In the village in Nepal, everyone is cared for and valued and plays a vital role. No one goes hungry, and everyone monitors one another's health, as there's no doctor in town. Someone fashions knee-high boots from tightly woven sheep and goat wool. Another person, who lives on the edge of town, is good at butchering meat. These specialty jobs are integral to the daily well-being of the entire population, which lives in near isolation, what feels like light-years away from a hospital, a department store, and the internet.

This revelation learned from village-based societies in the Himalayas brought about a radical shift in our thinking, seeing each member of a gift economy as a vital participant, no matter their social status or economic reality. Intrigued, we wondered, could we try this ourselves? And, more important, would it work? There are intact gift economies and giving cultures around the world, including the First Nations of the Pacific Northwest Coast and Salish Sea, the gemachim of Judaism, and the shared American tradition of passing along baby and children's clothes as hand-me-downs. Cooperative economies are ancient and have been with all of us in diverse forms throughout human history, yet many of us have never been exposed to, or don't recognize, this traditional way of sharing resources and strengthening ties between neighbors. There is a power and magic in a local-connection-centered sharing economy.

In today's society, we don't tend to have real social networks to rely upon, as Samdzong does, despite having virtual ones. We live like hermits, trying to survive on our own at all costs, our homes filled with items meant just for us. We wanted to bring this web of interconnectedness to our own home island. But would this even be possible?

The Importance of Having Something to Give

You don't need to travel halfway across the world or trek over high mountain passes to realize how much we can benefit from the power of giving in our own communities in a hyperconnected world.

While Liesl and her family were in the Himalayas, Rebecca and her children were at sea level, on an island in Puget Sound, having a very different sort of experience. Thanks to a sudden and jarring plunge into unemployed single parenthood during the Great Recession and without steady income, Rebecca found herself needing to feed and clothe three people. She signed up for food stamps, but this assistance wasn't enough to cover things such as fresh vegetables or fruit. Experiencing food insecurity (a plight that is all too common to single mothers and their children in the US) had a profound impact on Rebecca. Seemingly overnight, she struggled to regain her sense of dignity and sense of self-worth, while feeling isolated by her financial poverty amid her largely wealthy community.

A NOTE FROM REBECCA

My first few years as a single parent were staggering in their difficulty. I thought I was tired as the parent of five- and three-year-old daughters when I had a partner to help me raise them; raising my girls on my own burned through my second wind, then my third, and then settled me into a new normal in which the anxiety of my responsibilities, and my inability to meet them all, was ever present.

In the beginning, when I was rationing the gas in our car and learning how to stretch our monthly food stamp allowance, it dawned on me very quickly: we needed to find walkable entertainment and free food. At the end of our first lean winter, we were walking along a trail near our house when I spotted bitter cress coming up through the gravel. This is a plant that most people discard as a weed, and it's one of the very first free spring foods to emerge from the soil here. It has a crisp flavor, a bit like arugula. I taught my daughters how to carefully pull it up, catching each plant's full circle of lacy green branches. We filled our coat pockets and had our first fresh greens in weeks for dinner, a free salad that made us feel clever and healthy instead of just poor and hungry.

I needed more than those greens for nourishment; I needed the reminder that I had something to share: I didn't have money to buy the fresh vegetables my kids needed, but I had the knowledge to teach them how to find their own, and that was knowledge I could share beyond my family. Even when I couldn't buy gifts for others, I could find things to give.

Being unable to pay all of my own bills and being unable to feed my kids without help made me feel less worthy, less important in the world, like a burden on my friends and family. Even though I didn't believe these things about myself (or anyone else who was financially poor or dealing with scarcity), I couldn't escape the negative tape playing on a loop in my mind. My desire to build a local gift economy came from my desire to empower myself and others in my position to see how they were wealthy in other, more important ways than having money. I wanted a chance to give as well as to receive, as a way to reclaim my sense of worth within my community.

For me, the first gift economy Liesl and I created wasn't a hobby, it was how I fed and clothed my children and myself and, most important, how I regained a sense of myself as a person who deserved to have both needs and wants, and had the power to help others meet theirs. Sometimes our abundance is in tangible goods, sometimes it is in gifts of time, knowledge, or presence, and sometimes it's in teaching a neighbor which weeds are edible or sharing half of a pizza. It all counts equally in a gift economy.

An Economy Built on Giving

Our Western culture is based on capitalism and a market economy, drawing a stark line between those who have and those who don't. An item's known market value is of utmost importance, and people with spending money are able to purchase things much more easily. Because of this, there is great social value placed on amassing personal wealth and status in the form of brand-new or so-called luxury items, and many people associate the use of secondhand items with poverty and lack of social status. People who are struggling financially are bombarded with societal messages that their poverty is shameful, something to be hidden, and we internalize the message that only the financially well-off are "givers," while those with fewer resources are inherently "takers."

Moreover, the social connections we form aren't built around our homes and neighborhoods in the same way they used to be. We create social networks through work, schools, houses of worship, gyms, and other "third places" away from home. Many of us lead daily lives in which we hardly recognize our next-door or across-the-hall neighbors. People want to maintain their privacy, or, perhaps, they might want this connection but don't feel safe or comfortable initiating contact in person.

Despite the fact that we all have needs and wants, and an innate ability and desire to both give and receive, there are no prescribed ways to do this on equal footing, person to person. And this is contributing to an excess of stuff that's draining our bank accounts and natural resources. In any given neighborhood, there is a huge collection of things that are owned by individuals but could become shared resources. In a single community of fifty homes, there might be close to fifty complete sets of home tools, car seats for newborns and toddlers, toys for every stage of child development, cookbooks, plumbing snakes, clothing of every size and color, furniture, old monitors, camping gear, and so on. Sharing this bounty of stuff is not our ingrained cultural habit, and so our homes are filled to the brim with personal sets of everything that advertising has told us we need to fulfill our dreams, and everything we think we need to have in case times are tough and we find ourselves alone, needing to survive hardship.

What if each household stopped buying these things, and we shared more? Would we find things of value? Our original hope in launching the Buy Nothing Project was that by doing so, we would reduce our overall consumption and yet still meet our daily needs. By building social status through our generosity as givers and grace as recipients, we would each learn how to share, with trust, on an equal playing field. And most important, we would learn to trust that there is enough (stuff, bounty, human kindness) to go around.

The Samdzong village doesn't have a huge influx of new items because the people live far from any markets. Out of necessity, they live in close connection to the Earth and one another, their lifestyle rich in spiritual culture and interpersonal connectedness. They spend less time managing their stuff. The items that do make it into the village are used fully and communally, until they cannot be repurposed into anything else that's useful.

We realize life in a tiny village far from the comforts of our own suburban life is not easy, and we're not implying that we should all pick up and move to Nepal, but there are practical lessons we can learn from this remote village. We've held on tightly to this idealized image of the village gift economy, in hopes of replicating these ideas at home to strengthen our communities and learn to use and repurpose our tangible and intangible gifts in various ways. The seven steps in this book provide an outline for doing just that.

Starting with Step 1: Give. You will discover how to bond a little more closely with your neighbors, through sharing more of our things and ourselves. We've seen it happen, over and over. With a local giving culture, you won't have to buy things to feel joy, clothe your family, furnish your home, repair what's broken, or help others. You will begin to build a local culture that values sharing and communal use of stuff above individual collections held for solitary use. Buying Nothing might just get you everything if you follow the seven steps we offer in this book.

Step 1: Give

What is the single most important thing you can do to start your Buy Nothing life, to find joy, and get everything?

Give.

It may sound counterintuitive, but the act of giving is the first thing you can do to create this shift in your lifestyle. Giving puts you in the best position to seek items or services you'll want or need later on. If there's one thing we've learned from running a few thousand local gift economies, it's that giving is an action that brings people an immediate giddy joy, and joy is a solid foundation for building strong relationships. It's also a first step in helping someone near you reduce their consumption of resources. Giving what we already have is the superglue we need to bind us to a communal web of sharing that can have a more powerful impact on your life than any big-box store you've pushed a shopping cart through.

> **Conspicuous consumption isn't doing our planet any favors; conspicuous sharing is the antidote.**

In its purest anthropological sense, gift giving is a symbolic form of reciprocity that can help integrate each of us into society, ensuring we'll be cared for and guaranteeing our own role in improving the lot of others. Serial gift giving is akin to a political move, one that sparks unspoken obligation, creating a bond between giver and receiver, and integration of both into the greater good. This may sound like a lot of anthro-economic-ethno-enviro mumbo jumbo, but our experiment has borne out some truths that we've witnessed several hundred thousand times.

Through the simple act of offering up something you no longer need, indeed, something you may have considered throwing away, you'll both help the environment and improve your social standing. Conspicuous consumption isn't doing our planet any favors; conspicuous sharing is the antidote, a powerful tool for good, both social and environmental. Anonymous giving, as laudable as it is, doesn't necessarily provide much-needed binding social glue for a community.

When we set up our first Buy Nothing Project group, we chose Facebook as our platform because it was where people already were, where it's easy to see mutual friends you share with strangers, and where all of the giving could happen in full view of each group member. Being seen has a magic of its own, and these groups become digital versions of the tight-knit villages in the Himalayas that Liesl witnessed. Through our Buy Nothing experiment, we've learned a lesson that applies to all giving, online and in person: when a group of people witnesses giving, receiving, and sharing on a daily basis, it builds stronger connections among everyone, not just those on either end of each item or service being shared. There's a sense of collective joy that builds around watching gifts being given and received.

SHAINE'S BUY NOTHING STORY

You'll find these boxes throughout this book. Each one tells the story of a real-life person who is living la vida Buy Nothing. Here's Shaine's story, from our very own island community: "My friend asked me to Buy Nothing a stroller. So after leaving her place, I'm

> at the corner by the diner in my car and see a mom with a two-year-old boy and baby in [a] wrap. The two-year-old wouldn't hold Mom's hand, so she couldn't walk across the street. I rolled down my window and asked if she wanted this stroller I had in my back [seat]. She looked at me like I was crazy, but I looped around and pulled it out of the back of my car. I proceeded to tell her about Buy Nothing, gave her the stroller along with some Melissa & Doug [toy] stackables, and I explained this is how we do things here."
>
> —*Shaine Martin Schramling, Bainbridge Island*

This story from Shaine in the Pacific Northwest illustrates how to give with help from other people, and how to give in a way that fits seamlessly into your day to immediately and unexpectedly improve someone else's. Your public displays of giving don't have to be lavish. For women especially, giving can come so naturally (or in response to society's expectations and demands on us) that many of us may feel as if we have little left to give. This Buy Nothing experience is different. We are asking not for more rote giving, not for giving that leaves you feeling depleted, but for the sort of giving that comes from a place of abundance, giving that makes you feel powerful and respected. The *what* you give doesn't matter as much as the *why*. Experiment to find things and ways to give that make you feel good. There are many ways to reach this goal: When you give away items that you don't want anymore, you clear space in your home and can even let go of sad or upsetting memories along with the stuff, bringing a feeling of relief and a more open future. When you know your gift is going to improve a neighbor's life or bring them happiness, it brings you a sense of the power you have to improve the world around you.

Unlike some of the seemingly forced giving of time and resources that our lives often demand, your Buy Nothing giving is completely in your control. Set your own boundaries around your stuff and yourself, and give what and when you want. You get to choose the gifts, the recipients, the who, what, why, when, and how. There is sweetness for both giver and recipient when a gift is freely given and received without strings attached, between people who see each other as equally important. This is the sort of giving that Buying Nothing will empower you to discover and cultivate.

KITIYA'S BUY NOTHING STORY

"I thought I'd offer up something a little different today. This seemingly empty jar is filled with kindness. If you are in need of a little kindness right now, register your interest below. I will fill this jar with something that will hopefully make you smile just a little. The hope is that it will fill you with enough kindness that you will be able to fill this jar with your own kindness and pass it on to someone else who needs it."

—*Kitiya Dufall, Perth, Australia*

Kitiya Dufall takes a less immediately tangible approach to giving, proving the power of simplicity and imagination. Her post of a photo of a glass jar to her Western Australia gift economy along with this story generated goodwill and enthusiasm for creatively filling that jar with emblems of kindness. Much of the beauty of giving comes from interacting with real people who have real needs, desires, worries, thoughts, and feelings. You and your acquaintances are not ordering from an online company or dealing with a customer service operator across the country or halfway around the world. There's no money involved; no one is playing the role of buyer or seller. You're interacting with one another, bringing creative sharing into a very human realm.

How to Give

We want you to give whenever you can. If you feel you have nothing to give, pick a closet, drawer, or room and clean it out. Junk drawers are a great place to start because most people think of the stuff in there as, well, junk. Organize it and you won't call it your junk drawer anymore. Or start with something broken or missing a zipper that you know you won't mend. A good rule of thumb with clothing is if you haven't worn it in a year, give it away. If you don't know how to use a tool, pass it on. With food, if it's way past its expiration date, compost it (or give it to someone who composts or has chickens). And with children's toys, stash a few in a box for two months, and if your child doesn't ask for it during that time, give it away. Stash a few more in a box next month, and repeat.

We guarantee that cleaning out your space of unused and unwanted things will make you feel better. Try taking a before picture of the space you're tackling, in advance of your cleanout. Then set aside all of the things you no longer need in a reusable box (avoid that plastic trash bag because this ain't trash), and be sure to take an after photo of your beautiful new space and share the side-by-side transformation with friends. We know you may want to just get rid of the stuff in the box that you've purged, as quickly as possible. But this next step is what will bring you even more joy: offer these items to your friends, colleagues, family, and neighbors through your best giving network (at work, school, church, or down the hallway), or drop it at the end of the driveway with a note if you have to. Throw a clothing swap party after cleaning out your (and your family's) closets. It's a fun way to get friends and friends of friends together for a couple hours of picking out new-to-you clothes while also giving away what's no longer needed. Inevitably, people keep in mind what size you and your kids are, and informal clothes swapping continues for years.

RECOMMENDED READING

Having a hard time letting go of all that stuff? Get out Marie Kondo's *The Life-Changing Magic of Tidying Up* to help you sort through your stuff and find items to give. Figure out which T-shirts "bring you joy" and which carry baggage, and let go of the guilt that often comes with purging what we don't want or need.[2] We love her appreciation and respect for every item she handles, and now we want to take you by the hand and show you how each discard can bring you social capital and even more joy once it leaves your home. You can also use Margareta Magnusson's *The Gentle Art of Swedish Death Cleaning* to help you process and understand your emotions about parting with things you don't need or even want anymore but that you haven't been able to give away yet.[3] Kondo's method, which does wonders for sparking joy back into spaces of your home, can be your first step in finding the abundance you have to give to others. Likewise, Magnusson's method helps us clarify which stuff matters to us for the lives we're living, freeing us to move on from past versions of ourselves.

What makes Buying Nothing different from other methods isn't the purging, it's what comes next; we want to bring the special magic of giving into your life. Once you've got your pile of giveaways from your closets, shelves, and drawers, don't toss them! Don't be so quick to donate your unwanted things to a charity to give to someone you'll never have a chance of meeting. If we see our unwanted things as a gateway to connecting us to our community, to empowering one another to avoid buying new stuff and influencing manufacturers to produce only what is truly needed, we're doing something good for ourselves, others nearby, and the environment, too. The decluttering trend has increased donations at charities, more than they are able to sell, which is causing more stuff to end up in landfills. We have the power to turn our stuff into common assets, put it to good use in our cities and towns, giving our once-loved things a better fate than a trip to the dump.

Some people are hesitant to give, worried that their gifts might not be good enough, or that no one will want them. We get it; it's uncomfortable to try something new, and it can be intimidating to put yourself out there. If this is you, try to embrace this insecurity and think of this as an exercise meant to bring you closer to others. Remember, everyone loves a gift. And you can always use humor to cover up your anxieties about giving. Tackle your kids' toy chest and purge the preschool toys your littles have outgrown; they can go to good use in another family. Pass on your excess stash of herbal teas that never actually made you feel sleepy, zingy, or stress-free; admit defeat and get rid of that exercise bike you've rarely used. Cook a pot of soup and you'll make instant friends. People won't judge you if you're honest about what you're giving and the condition it's in. If you have a story that goes with it, tell it; everyone loves a good story as a means to connect them to an item.

Neeti Madan, a literary agent who lives in New York City, has a downstairs neighbor in Manhattan who is a single mom who moved into Neeti's building a few years ago. The new neighbor's son is a few years younger than Neeti's. Rather than leaving his train tracks on the "free" shelf in the building, where someone anonymous would have picked them up, Neeti's son chose to give his tracks directly to the younger boy, knowing he'd enjoy them. "It was much more gratifying to watch him show her son how to put together the tracks," Neeti shared with us. "We've ended up being friendly enough now that we were the door she knocked on when she had a severe allergic reaction and needed to leave her son with someone, and she also joined us for our annual Christmas tree trimming festivities."

Give. Give creatively and often. Give freely, without any strings attached, for the pure joy of it. We promise it will bring you closer to those around you and prepare you for the next step in Buying Nothing: asking.

DARIA'S BUY NOTHING STORY

"Truthfully, having FULL trust in my community to come through and gift anything I may ever need if I ever had another child is what truly gives me the freedom to give away everything the moment my daughter's not using it anymore. I gift clothing and toys the moment we outgrow them, I gift leftover food and anything that has been sitting unused in my garage or my own closet, on countertops, tucked away in cabinets. I've literally gifted my daughter's dirty laundry when I knew she'd outgrow the clothes before I could pack them and unpack them as we were preparing to move. This mind-set of trust and interdependence within my Buy Nothing community has shifted so much about how I see the things I use in my life."

—*Daria Kelsey, a member of the Buy Nothing Global Team, our inner core of project leaders, Tacoma, Washington*

Regarding Gift Economies, Women, Poverty, and Wealth

We like to remind ourselves that the word *economy* comes from the Greek word *oikos*, which means "household." While women have historically been disenfranchised from ownership and leadership in the commercial market economy, we are the original stewards of the first economy—households. Economic models from spheres traditionally controlled by women haven't been seen as legitimate models for mainstream commerce, academia, and politics, but these mom-economies tend to be inclusive of others, mindful of resources, noncompetitive, and fair at their core.[4] We can attest to the fact that the majority of our more than six thousand volunteers in the Buy Nothing Project (to the tune of at least 95 percent) are women. This is not surprising to us, as we believe women tend to be the managers of the materials that come and go from most homes. We pack it in, we pack it out.

We have helped local volunteers set up local gift economies in dozens of countries so far, covering the full range of socioeconomic, racial, ethnic, religious, cultural, and political diversity. Every neighborhood around the world has access to the same abundance of generosity, no matter the average income level or financial health. We are basing this on direct learned experience and observation. When members of less affluent neighborhoods express concern that "there won't be good stuff" or "enough of it" in their local neighborhood to start a Buy Nothing group, this has been disproved time and again. There is no neighborhood devoid of gifts, no community with a poverty of kindness or mutual caring. In fact, we frequently see gift economies in areas that know financial poverty grow more quickly than those where the majority of residents are financially wealthy. Building a new giving culture or nourishing an intact, existing one is work that every one of us can be a full and equal participant in. The most valuable gifts we've seen are the gifts of human connection, gifts of service and self, gifts of knowledge, time, expertise, and other intangibles; these can be the most life-changing, and they're gifts we each have the power to give and to receive.

When it comes to giving, you cannot go wrong. We offer our top tips and ideas in this book for giving in ways that quickly effect profound change, but there is no wrong way to give. There is no gift too large, and no gift too small. Give your giving as much thought as you'd like, setting boundaries around yourself and your stuff, to give in ways that improve your life while your gifts are improving other lives. The majority of participants in the Buy Nothing Project are women, which isn't surprising because studies show that women tend to be more generous than men. According to *Money* magazine, the difference may be explained by our motivations: women tend to believe that helping others brings us greater happiness than spending money on ourselves, and women are also more likely to define success by generosity toward others as opposed to our personal wealth.[5] We're not suggesting, however, that women give at the expense of our own well-being, or at the cost of our personal boundaries.

Studies also show that low-income people are more "prosocial," meaning they're less selfish and typically share more, out of compassion. Dr. Paul Piff, a psychologist at the University of California, Irvine, who has studied generosity in people of differing socioeconomic strata, explained in an interview to NPR that "the main variable that we find that consistently explains this differential pattern of giving and helping and generosity among the upper and lower class is feelings of sensitivity and care for the welfare of other people and, essentially, the emotion that we call compassion."[6] Tap into your compassion when you give, but be mindful of your boundaries. Don't give if the gift will hurt you or your family financially or if it will add unpleasant pressure to your schedule for the day. Give when it fits fluidly into your day, not when it's burdensome on any level. But please suspend any fear you may have about scarcity, and trust that there is enough to go around. As Daria's story demonstrates, it's easy to give when you know in your heart that there's so much bounty around us, you can give something away today and ask for a replacement whenever you need one from your sharing community.

When you give, experiment with a variety of ways or stick to just one; give quickly and all at once or slowly and one tiny item at a time. Give out loud or give silently; it doesn't matter how you do it, just give. All giving is good giving.

How to Create a Gift Economy Group

If you don't have a local gift economy group to join, you can create your own:

1. Create a giving culture or gift economy by announcing your intention and inviting people to join in. Host a monthly gifts and food potluck, or get the word out by posting a flyer in your favorite local coffee shop or gathering spot, or via email, group text, a social media platform, or any other means.
2. Do the same at work, at school, or at your place of worship. Gather together a core group of givers and receivers and ask them to invite their friends into the giving group.
3. Encourage interested people to meet at a public park weekly to share what each has in abundance.
4. Use your personal social media as a place to regularly post gifts for local friends and ask for what you need. Model this, and others will follow your example.
5. Create a free box at the end of your driveway, building entry, or in the communal space of your apartment building.
6. Find a local coffee shop, train station, or gathering place that would be open to having a free box where locals could share items.
7. Put out a basket of excess produce at your community

garden, and add other items to it, inviting others to do the same.

8. Ask your public library if they'll allow for a bulletin board gift economy where people can post asks and gives and expressions of gratitude.

9. Public swimming pools can have boxes set up as a "free store." The pool near us has a selection of bathing suits, towels, and clothing for those who need them.

10. Farmers' markets and dog parks are other venues for daily or weekly sharing, too.

11. Start a quick giving session at the end of your book group, school and community meetings, or your knitting circle.

Many of us know very little about our neighborhoods. They're zones we travel through as we make our way from the privacy of our homes to wherever we need to be each day. We are either too busy to connect more or perhaps too addicted to our smartphones and social media. Many of us no longer spend time being physically present in our communities, reaching out to the people around us. Instead, we log hours on our devices, connecting with contacts far away. Each of our social infrastructures has grown into virtual online communities that are quickly replacing the real-world, face-to-face interactions we used to have daily with neighbors.

The past six years of launching Buy Nothing has taught us that the legendary village of the past, where gift economies flourished, isn't entirely lost. They're still here, born out of necessity, human social evolution, and love, high in the Himalayas and in other areas with uninterrupted gift economy cultures. But they are also right here, in our own communities, and can often be facilitated by those very things that get such a bad rap. Why not take social media and smartphones and put them to work for us, creating in-person human connection? Using your personal accounts online to offer gifts to your social network does just this. We're working on our own free global gift economy app, **Soop**.app (**S**hare **O**n **O**ur **P**latform), and hope you'll join us there.

MYRA'S BUY NOTHING STORY

"From the first day, I have envisioned myself falling backward into the hands of this community, and letting go—knowing full well I will be 'caught.' It has been with this premise that I have found the courage to let go—giving AND receiving. I encourage everyone to 'let go.' You will be surprised and rewarded in more ways than you can imagine. Do not hesitate to ask or give. It is what makes us human."

—*Myra Zocher, Bainbridge Island*

Still hesitant? Perhaps you think you have nothing to share. Believe us, you have plenty to give. Trust, as Myra suggests, that your giving will be accepted and will begin to weave a safety net around your entire community as your gifts inspire others to do the same. A pure gift economy values each member equally as a giver and a receiver. We're all integral to the overall health of the whole, and each of our gifts has the same value. What might be worthless to you, indeed what you think is trash, could be an invaluable asset to someone next door. Imagine the surprise our friend Matthew Clemente got when he agreed to post in his local Buy Nothing Project group the gift of a nonfunctioning prosthetic leg on behalf of a friend who didn't want to throw it out. Within a few hours he had responses, one of which was from a University of Washington professor who said she'd love to have the prosthetic leg for components for her class, because she teaches prosthetics. One person's trash is truly another's treasure . . .

Gift of Self

STEPH'S BUY NOTHING STORY

"I grew up in Hamilton, moved out, came back, moved out, and resettled here after losing everything I owned in Hurricanes Irma and Maria on St. Thomas. My entire cottage, now, is furnished with Buy Nothing and thrift store finds. Not only that, but I have met wonderful people. I just finished taking someone I met through the group for his daily radiation treatments for five weeks."

—*Steph Moffat, local volunteer for Buy Nothing Hamilton-Wenham, Massachusetts*

If you're still stumped and feel you have nothing to give, try this: What talent, ability, or assistance can you share? Gifts of self are the most touching gifts you can give, and perhaps the most difficult, because they require you to give something that isn't material but a part of you, your personality, and requires your presence and care. Without question, these are the most meaningful and long-lasting gifts that have the greatest impact. These gifts don't need to be complicated. Steph's gift of transportation and company for her neighbor undergoing chemotherapy didn't require a specialized skill to have huge impact.

We encourage you to try your hand at giving a little something of yourself to others. What comes easily to you that someone else might struggle to accomplish? Give that. Are you good at cleaning out a fridge? Are you an excellent editor? Do you love gardening? Do you have a truck? Can you wash windows or mop a floor? Do you love to take portraits? Can you cut hair? Are you a great cook? Do you have room in your sailboat for another person to join you? Can you fix a bike's flat tire? Do you know a lot about local wild mushrooms? Do you love to play board games? Do you have excellent organizational skills? Can you teach someone to knit or sew? You see where we're headed with this.

JILL'S BUY NOTHING STORY

"Offer: In-person fitted sheet folding lesson.

I was trying to think of something nontangible I could offer. I am an 'expert' fitted sheet folder. My mom taught me at a young age and I've been doing it ever since. If there is any interest I could reserve a room at the library."

—*Jill Smulson, Elkridge, Maryland*

Jill's offer was met with such a positive response that she reserved a room at her local library for a free fitted sheet folding clinic to teach this mysterious art.

Dream up your gift of self and offer it to your community. You'll gain further connection and a feeling of satisfaction, knowing you've done something extraordinary that will impact others, even if it's just transportation to the supermarket for someone who needs a ride. Go forth and do what humans do best: give! Take note of how it goes, whom you meet, and how it makes you feel.

We Invite You to Give

Here's where you bring Buy Nothing *giving* to life. We invite you to give three things away.

Your first gift will be an item with a simple story. Pick a piece of clutter from your home, something that's been rattling around the trunk of your car, or stashed in the back corner of a drawer. Something that has a story like this: "I have three half-cup measures! I only need one. I would like to find new homes for two of them. I have no idea how I acquired so many, and they have no special place in my heart. Who can use one? What will you bake?"

Your second gift will be a gift of self. You can keep it easy and offer up something you've made (no one ever has trouble finding a willing recipient of a home-baked cookie, or a warm meal), but we hope you'll try for something even more personal: If you like to bake, pick a recipe that reminds you of a special person and pass along a story about them, including the recipe and your baked offering. If you're crafty, offer to make something (knit a scarf in someone's favorite colors, crochet a soft washcloth for a baby or senior citizen). If you're handy, offer to fix something broken or build something new. If you have a hobby or day job skill that you enjoy, offer up your knowledge or creations: sewing, painting, gardening, reading aloud, sending encouraging notes or emails, writing poems, singing, walking with someone, sharing a favorite city walk or little-known park, taking a trip to a museum, mowing a lawn, shoveling snow, playing cards, giving a pedicure, organizing a pantry. We've seen all of these and more. The gift itself isn't important. The key here is to select a gift of self that will bring you pleasure, not something that will seem grueling or burdensome. Turn something you'd love to do regardless into a gift for another person so that there's enjoyment all around in the giving and receiving. If you have a secret skill or interest, something your friends don't know about, we hope you'll find a way to share it as a gift of self, to expand your genuine presence in your community so that people begin to see and appreciate your full self.

Your third gift will be an item that has a meaningful story and that you no longer want. This may be something with good memories that you would like to see extend its joyful reach into the world. Or perhaps it's something that has more complicated, bittersweet, or even painful memories around it, and you'd like to see it move along to a new steward to create a happier chapter, which will in turn shift the object's meaning to you, offering a chance to pull some new happiness, release, or resolution through the act of giving.

Giving away your old wedding dress, for instance, is a way of honoring your happy marriage, wrapping a new bride in this garment of love, or it can help to produce something positive from the sorrow of a marriage that has ended. There are many such objects in our homes: inherited dishes and furniture, books with inscriptions in handwriting we don't want to see again, gifts from former beloveds, strange tchotchkes from great-aunts. Take a look around and find something that has a story you'd like to tell, be it happy, sad, or something else entirely, but a story that has some meaning to you, a connection to your history. This gift is two things together as a package deal—your item and your story. Be sure to give both, in whatever form you like (no need to write a book or even an essay; stories can be told by voice, scribbled on a notecard, or shared in any other form that pleases you, the teller).

Once you have selected your gifts, decide how you'd like to offer them. Remember, you are in charge of your giving, and all giving is good giving: you can offer these gifts up to a large group of people, or you can select possible recipients per whatever criteria matter to you. Make a list of what, to whom, when, and where you'd like to give, and you've penciled out your own gift economy!

To make this shift even more fun and successful, start with a group of friends or coworkers. Join our worldwide discussion forum at buynothinggeteverything.com to get the support you need from others working on this same challenge. You'll find a welcoming community of people eager to share ideas and expand the basic ideas we offer here. Talk about it in person and send out emails or flyers to build your own personalized local sharing network.

BAYAN'S BUY NOTHING STORY

"I have learned to be a little brave. You knock on a door, you don't know what's on the other side. I think the giving group brings out the good in people. We are all human, all the same."

—*Bayan Kazem, Winnipeg, Manitoba*[7]

STEP 2: ASK

Most of us have difficulty asking for what we want and need. Why is that? Living in a society that celebrates independence and autonomy means that many of us have internalized the message that to expose our vulnerability, needs, and desires is to betray an inner weakness that can be perceived as failure. Self-actualized people don't need other people, right? We aspire to have the means to acquire all the resources we may need or want in our lives, even at the expense of others. Gift economies are built on the core assumption that there is enough to go around and that if we share what we have with one another, this sharing will build relationships between us, relationships that will protect us, support us, provide for us, and magnify our joy. No person is an island. We experience so much more joy when we are connected to others in times of both plenty and want.

A member in one of our first groups in Washington State posted an ask for fresh flowers from local gardens to place around the room when his wife returned from the hospital to enter hospice care in their home. When she arrived home for the last time, there were buckets and vases of flowers lining her front porch, donated and arranged by strangers, meant to surround her with natural beauty, fragrance, and kindness as she transitioned out of this life. Requests like this—those that require vulnerability in asking— also reap powerful rewards that are felt by recipients as well as givers, and they become local stories that guide a neighborhood's culture of compassion.

Money Separates Us, Gift Economies Connect Us

Perhaps there's no such thing as an original idea. As we struggled to articulate our philosophy, we stumbled upon the writings of author and gift economy advocate Charles Eisenstein and discovered a validation, in his writings, that indicates we may be on the right track. It took us a few years to learn, by observing hundreds of healthy gift economies, that money isn't all that wonderful. As Eisenstein suggests, it separates us. The market economy begets isolation, and money disconnects us from one another. When we pay for something, we have no lasting obligation to the seller and are disconnected from the person who made, grew, or inherited the item. Similarly, if you pay someone for their service, you have no obligation to each other, except for the payment and the service. You're less inclined to connect with them because the relationship is defined by a monetary transaction. The money in the equation limits our roles and establishes a barrier to connection as equals. Compounding this, the market economy is built upon a model of scarcity. With the assumption of limited supply, we're led to believe that there's not enough to go around, so we compete with one another for the same resources, thinking, "More for you is less for me."[1] We become divided, each of us out to get more than the next.

> The money economy also destroys community, replacing gift interactions with paid services and casting us into a world of strangers. Because it is fundamentally competitive, it also creates the experience of a hostile world in which no one cares.[2]
>
> —*Charles Eisenstein*

By contrast, the gift economy operates around a premise of abundance, an assurance that if you give something away, you aren't losing it forever. There will always be more of that item if you need it again. There's also a value inherent in giving: your gift connects you to someone else and enriches their lives. Often, the gift has a story attached to it, and that story becomes a part of our collective narrative, yet another gift. The story acts like glue and we tell it over and over because it makes us feel good. In turn, we learn something about the giver and the recipient.

Just like giving, asking begets connection. The ask, and the act of receiving, is the critically important other half of the gift economy equation. Asking requires trust, courage, a willingness to show our vulnerability, and faith that our requests will not diminish our value or respect in the eyes of others. In truth, our requests foster interdependence that benefits us all.

But, let's face it, asking is one of the most difficult steps many of us will take in this Buy Nothing challenge. For women especially, stating our needs can make us feel vulnerable and exposed. Why is that? Many of us believe it shows weakness or disrespect. Traditionally, women have been socialized to be selfless and nice, and nice girls don't ask for what they want. Nice girls accept whatever they are given, no matter how it lines up with their true wants or desires. Studies have shown us that women often don't get what we want and deserve, simply because we don't ask.[3] We have been taught that it is our job to *give*, not to *get*. Girls and women are often brought up to be the caretakers in society and therefore have difficulty, even shame in, expressing our own needs, suppressing them in order to achieve what society holds as our greatest potential: helping others. Perhaps this is what makes women so good at asking for others yet so reticent to ask for things we want or need for ourselves. When we ask for something another person needs, we recognize the fairness of this request. Participating in Buying Nothing reminds us that everyone deserves to receive gifts—yes, every single one of us. This means you, too.

Many of us have also learned by experience that asking for things gives other people some form of power over us: we become reliant on someone else, or beholden to them. Too often, "gifts" of this kind—whatever form they take, such as when a date pays for dinner or when we ask for a raise—are given with strings attached. This is partly because in the market economy, the people with gifts to give are often people who also have more power than we do.

Gift economies can upend these gift-power connections. There are no strings attached when a gift is given freely. When asking and giving happens publicly in a gift economy, there are no longer hidden strings to pull. And when everyone asks for things, we all see the truth: none of us is entirely self-sufficient, we all have things we want and need that we cannot create for ourselves, and there is no shame in this.

Think of this: When a friend asks you for something, do you think any less of them? Of course not. We usually feel grateful to be able to give to those who ask. Our aim is to help you see that asking is not just a strength, it's a virtue, one that is required to set off a chain reaction of giving.

We've Forgotten How to Ask

We are out of practice asking for things, which is why many Buy Nothing members say that *asking* is one of the hardest things— it's much easier and less complicated to just give than to make yourself vulnerable by *asking* for what you need. In his book *Sacred Economics*, Charles Eisenstein explains how averse many of us are to that feeling of obligation, or gratitude: "We don't want to receive gifts because we don't want to be obligated to anyone. We don't want to owe anybody anything. We don't want to depend on anyone's gifts or charity—'I can pay for it myself, thank you. I don't need you.'"[4]

This instinct to buy rather than ask is costing us, quite literally. Credit card debt hit a record high in the US at the end of 2018, averaging about $8,284 for the average American household.[5] We outfit our homes with the same items, drive our cars to the same schools, the same stores and events, without rolling down the windows to notice who might live next door. We're cloistered in our autonomy, paying for everything ourselves, and are seemingly self-sufficient. And meanwhile, manufacturers drain our natural resources to produce more things for the disconnected citizens who seek to fill the void with stuff.

A Buy Nothing Wedding

But once you take the leap to embrace a mentality of asking instead of buying, the extraordinary can happen. We've seen brave asks create beautiful outcomes time and again. One of the most extraordinary examples of this is the Buy Nothing wedding. There have been many over the years, and this kind of neighbor-sourced celebration becomes a particularly intimate experience for all involved, as the communal participation creates a rich web of giving and receiving.

In some instances, Buy Nothing weddings are a great example of how a circumstance of lack can turn into one of abundance, a generous microcosm of giving and asking that can bring about true joy and bonding beyond the guest list. Hosting a wedding is not only daunting, but it can be cost prohibitive. Buy Nothing weddings are both a throwback to earlier and simpler times, and a way to bypass the wedding industrial complex. This often starts with the dress, which is borrowed or given. (Many married women have their wedding dresses hanging in closets, never to be worn again. Offering your dress to a bride-to-be can be the first step in planting the seed for a Buy Nothing wedding.) But other traditional wedding needs and highlights can also be freely given: potluck food and wine, a beautiful backyard, tables and chairs, hairdressing, a justice of the peace, a string quartet, candles, decorations, a vintage car.

Buy Nothing Project participant Markessa Pinder grew up in foster homes until her grandmother adopted her when Markessa was twelve. At twenty-seven, after fleeing an abusive boyfriend, she rekindled a relationship with her true love and they planned to marry. Markessa assumed she'd have a simple wedding at city hall, with two friends as witnesses, because she and her fiancé wanted to save for school and a house. But Markessa didn't have a dress to wear for the occasion. She asked in her Buy Nothing group in Kirkland, Washington, to borrow "just a basic party dress, anything to look pretty."

Robyn Dosono, a member of the group whom Markessa had never met, had a dressy dress for her, but she also wondered why Markessa wasn't having a more formal wedding celebration, rather than a courtroom wedding. Markessa privately messaged Robyn back, saying that she had no family and few friends in the area. "Money's big. Weddings are expensive and having a baby with two older kids, there's other dreams, ya know," Markessa later told the local news.[6]

Robyn immediately posted in the Kirkland group, asking if anyone wanted to help the couple put on a dream wedding. "I just didn't have a mom, so she came through," Markessa explained, through tears. Within seven hours of Robyn's post, the couple had a donated venue, a wedding photographer and videographer, a gown and bridesmaids' dresses, tables, chairs, roses and hydrangeas, personalized wedding favors, gourmet dishes for the buffet-style dinner, and a DJ to host the festivities. The gifts offered up by strangers just kept coming: one woman went through a junk drawer and gleefully offered a wedding ring from her husband's previous marriage. It was a community celebration that would've cost at least $10,000 that turned into an excuse to celebrate how love and sharing of our talents and time can triumph over buying things. "This was them asking for a cup of sugar and they got the cake and the steak and the lobster, too!" said participant Carol Myers.

Buy Nothing Project member Erika O'Leary of the Beacon Hill neighborhood in Seattle also had a gift economy wedding. For her it was a chance to bring meaning to her wedding because most of her friends were people whom she had met in her local gift economy. According to the *Seattle Times*, which profiled the wedding, Erika "threw a 'Buy Nothing wedding' with a donated dress, cake, décor, flowers, an American Sign Language interpreter for deaf relatives, and a wedding photographer. Her biggest outlay was $300 for the venue."[7] A wedding, on average, can easily cost $30,000, but because participants pitch in, gift economy weddings are more about everyone sharing in the rite of passage.

Step 2: Ask

We've introduced the Buy Nothing challenge, where you don't buy anything for a week or longer. Maybe you haven't felt the need to buy anything anyway. But maybe you have: Is there something you want or think you need to make a trip to the store for? Is there an item that could be repaired, or something you simply need help with? Make a list of these needs. Then ask your neighbors or members of your giving group for that donut baking tray, ladder, or help repairing your grandmother's old lamp.

Go ahead: ask! It's time to get out of your comfort zone and just ask already! This is the biggest hurdle stopping you from connecting with your neighbors, friends, and coworkers, and jumping fully and freely into the giving networks around you. Modeling this behavior will show others that they can also ask for what they want.

People love to share what comes easily to them. Some people like to weed gardens and help organize closets, others love to make chili, some find it effortless to edit CVs, while others enjoy driving and are happy to provide rides. These are some examples of the kinds of things we can do for someone else. Think about something you'd love to get done, but always felt you needed to hire someone to help you with, and get out there and ask for the help—for free. Someone will likely be happy you asked.

Christine, a young mom living in a northern suburb of Detroit, drew up the courage to ask for something she never dreamed would come true: the gift of accrued airline miles for a flight to Korea. Christine was born in Korea but grew up in Michigan with her adopted family. Earlier that year she had reconnected with her biological family in South Korea and wanted to meet them for the first time. Christine's request gave a stranger the chance to give excess miles for her life-changing trip. Christine wrote, in gratitude, "This gifting group has given me a trip to South Korea to visit my biological family for the first time. I'm overwhelmed right now thinking that this trip now has a countdown for a date in the fall. When I was looking at flights and contemplating travel over 6,000 miles . . . (I thought of the tenets of the Buy Nothing group) No ask has a value greater than another. Any ask is important. All asks are worthy of asking. And so I asked. I never dreamed that this ask would be fulfilled. I put it out to the universe, and the universe sent me our neighbor.

"Our neighbor, Kristy, was very unselfish to take time away from a very demanding time in her life right now to secure this flight for me. She reminds us all that no ask is too great and, most importantly to me right now, that our community is here to support each other in our journeys. Her gift to me is beyond airline miles. It is beyond a monetary value. Friends, this gift is an opportunity, memories to be made, reconciliation of identity, and a level of understanding about my past and history that I have never known before. We all have gifts. Kristy's gift is love. She gave this gift to a neighbor that is a stranger."

The feel-good meter for Christine's giving network in Michigan hit the roof as every member got a good dose of just how powerful gift giving can be. One neighbor, whose son had taught in Korea, even offered to provide Christine with popular gifts from the US that she knew would be well loved in Korea, like baseball items, to take to her family.

As Lissa Jagodnik, one of our original volunteers from the Seattle area who worked on the infrastructure of the Buy Nothing Project to help make it a worldwide network, explains, Buying Nothing is similar to that American tradition of bringing homemade cookies to new neighbors, as a way to welcome them to the neighborhood: "That neighbor wasn't standing at your door with a warm plate of chocolate chip cookies because they thought you needed cookies, or because they thought the children in the house were too thin. They were standing at the door with a warm plate of cookies because they wanted to meet their new neighbors; they wanted to get to know the people who just moved in; they wanted to feel good about introducing themselves. A local gift economy offers everyone the opportunity to knock on a neighbor's door (literally or figuratively) with a warm plate of cookies, a chance to introduce themselves, a way to get to know one another. This is our primary goal. It's really not about the 'cookies.' It's not about who has more or who has less, who needs more and who needs less, or the value of the gifts offered or received. It's about making connections, helping people feel welcome, and sharing not only our material goods but also our selves."

ALEXA'S BUY NOTHING STORY

"I used to think that caring for the environment meant deprivation. As I started to gift, I told the stories about what I was gifting. This necklace belonged to my grandmother. This magnifying glass was fun for my brother and me to check out caterpillars and toads. One neighbor gifted her bras, which she could no longer wear after a double mastectomy. These stories opened doors, quite literally. After asking for a French press, I found myself in my neighbor's living room, her kids shoving their kitty in my face and telling me all about her funny behaviors and what they were doing in school. Neighbors began talking to neighbors, jump-started by the initial gifting of goods.

"In August 2017, I had the scare of my life. On the first day of a new job, I fell trying to catch the bus, breaking my hand and foot. Worse, I was moving that week from one walk-up to another. I couldn't walk, drive, type, write, dress myself, or hardly perform any physical task. In a desperate appeal, I told my Buy Nothing group. Immediately, neighbors lined up to drive me to doctor's appointments and deliver homemade meals. They packed and unpacked boxes, moved furniture, cleaned, did my laundry, and lent me a knee scooter.

"The neighborhood is a completely different place for me now. The people living among me are not strangers, but family. When we put connection first, and put people over profit, the results are kindness and gratitude. In abundance."

—*Alexa Carey, English professor in Connecticut and Buy Nothing Global Team member*

If you can't think of a service you need or something that needs fixing, double down and try your hand at asking for some "thing" that you need or want. Examples include that proverbial cup of sugar, rain boots for your daughter, a leash for your pup, a dinner you can freeze for a future night off from cooking, anything that's on your shopping list. We've seen requests met for prom dresses, firewood, wedding photographers, dog sitters, pianos, laptops, moving boxes, power drills, baby gates, pencils, stainless to-go coffee mugs, down jackets, and rides to the airport.

When one gift economy member was feeling homesick and a little depressed from the outcome of an important election, she decided to reach out for intangible gifts. Here was her request: "My ask is anything funny, awesome, beautiful, weird in the way of GIFs, stories, awesome blogs, links to music, etc., to make the next day or so a bit brighter and better mental health–wise." The gifts of funny memes, gorgeous photography, beautiful personal stories, links to enriching blogs and podcasts, as well as hundreds of distracting silly jokes she received to her social media account buoyed her through a tough time. We see similar requests being met every day in gift economies and personal conversations around the world. The gift of kindness and attention is always welcome. There's a reason cat videos are such a popular share.

All Gifts Have Equal Value

There are a couple of important unspoken rules in a gift economy: First, all gifts have equal value. We don't monetize them. A truckload of wood for heating a home may have just as much value to someone as a power cord for a laptop. We can't and don't put a dollar value on any gifts in a gift economy. The connections made, of course, are priceless. Second, the assumption is that our gift to you will not have a price tag put on it so you can then sell it back into the market economy, unless you disclose this intention at the get-go, when asking for the gift. Most of us will assume that each gift is freely given, freely taken, and will not be turned immediately into cash. There's a reason for this.

Early on in the Buy Nothing Project experiment, we discovered a few people were quietly reselling gifts given to them by other group members. They were, in essence, converting the gifts they received into cash. It rocked the very foundation of our social experiment, irking givers to the point they'd turn on the reseller in a witch hunt, emotions high with a deep sense of betrayal. Why did people feel so strongly about someone who resold their free gifts for money?

The health of a gift economy relies on giving, asking, and gratitude. But there's a hidden assumption that gifts must not be monetized or put in a hierarchy of value. If we did this, we would all compete for what the market defines as the most valuable gifts.

Our own sense of value for certain gifts would disappear, and there would be a scramble for the pricey items, while the less valued ones would sit unwanted, most likely ending up in the landfill.

In a healthy gift economy, it is also assumed a gift will be used as it is by the recipient, and not "cashed out." A gift economy is the antidote to a cash economy, antithetical to converting kindness into coins. When times are truly tough, we can ask for exactly what we need, rather than money. Instead of secretly reselling gifts to get money for a new winter coat, for instance, we can simply ask for the coat from the start. A Buy Nothing mind-set shifts us from putting monetary value on things and asks us to be honest; when we are sharing with our neighbors, honesty and full disclosure build trust, and trust is priceless.

The same goes for asks. No ask, in a true gift economy, is too great or too small. A good experiment to conduct in any of your giving groups is to ask members to make both a big ask and a small ask. Have everyone write them down and offer them to the group, or if you don't have a giving group, take a chance and post them on your social media accounts, or in places where your work or social community will see them. Put them out there, as an example, and ask others to do the same. This experiment in asking is the perfect illustration of how a nonmonetized giving culture can flourish and teach us how something considered "big" (i.e., of more value) to you may be a small and inconsequential thing to another, something they'd happily give you. What one person considers an important thing that they'd love to receive, like help in repairing a refrigerator, is often an easy request to fulfill by another. We've seen gifts like cars, boats, and housing asked for and received as well as gifts like catnip, newspapers, and empty shoeboxes.

BIG ASK, LITTLE ASK

In a Buy Nothing group in Silver Spring, Maryland, local admin Elisa Ferrante encouraged her group members to take part in a big ask/little ask exercise. She wrote, "I want to challenge each of you to think of something small that you would probably buy this week, something so small that you wouldn't think to ask for it—and ask for it here! (Who knows if someone will have it to give to you, maybe they will!) And then . . . think of something big that you would love to receive in your wildest dreams, something so big that you wouldn't think to ask for it—and ask for it here! (Who knows if someone will have it to give you, maybe they will!)"

Within minutes, the first person to chime in and participate was Anna Carson: "What a fun idea! My big ask is for a kayak, I've been wanting one since I moved to MD seven years ago, and hope to use it on the Anacostia to pick up bottles and trash on my rides. Small ask is for girls' hair bows. Thank you all for reading!"

A few minutes later another member, Dana, responded, "Anna Carson, I have so many girls' hair bows that my daughter refuses to wear! Happy to gift them to you."

Then, moments later, the big surprise came from neighbor Kelli Cronin: "Anna Carson, I have a blow-up kayak that I've been gathering the courage to get rid of. It would be easier if I knew you would be happy to use it!"

Anna responded, with gratitude, and in shock at how easy it was, "Thank you so much, Kelli!!! I would love it and promise to clean up local waterways while I'm paddling!! I feel like I just won the lottery!"

Yes, gift economies can save us money, but more important, they help us take money out of the equation. "Your money is no good here," we often say, because in an economy of sharing, money has no value. It's the act of giving and asking that has the most value. We can blur the lines between the haves and have-nots and put us all on equal footing. The gift economy helps us to move from thinking, "More for you is less for me," to "More for you is more for me." Or, even better yet, our ultimate goal: "More for you is more for us all."

In a giving culture, money has no value.

Unexpected Connections

There are also the unintended consequences of asking for what we want. When we go to pick that item up, we might be surprised by whom we meet. For Jaime Rosier, who lives near Los Angeles, the act of asking for and then receiving an item literally changed her life. A couple in her gift economy offered a gift she wanted, and she arranged to pop by for a quick pickup. Jaime was headed to a concert and was short on time. The couple convinced her to come in for a glass of wine and introduced her to their friend who was visiting. It was a lovely short visit, but Jaime's concert ticket wasn't going to wait, so she said her goodbyes over their protests. She headed home with her gift, only to realize she'd rather be back with these neighbors than at any concert.

Two days later, she found herself back there again to pick up another gift, and as fate would have it, their friend was also there again. They all hung out for hours, Jaime becoming fast friends with their best friend, and they exchanged numbers to keep in touch. "Mind you, I was single and ready to mingle, and he was handsome, intelligent, hilarious, adventurous, and a gentle-spirited man," recalls Jaime.

So when she got a text from her new friend, it led to their first date, quickly followed by a second, and they haven't stopped see-ing each other since. "Almost a year later, and my heart was stolen by this incredibly loving, kind, silly, creative, thoughtful gentle-man of a man, I'm over the moon to share that he asked me to marry him, and I said, 'I'd love to!'"

We have heard this kind of story thousands of times over: peo-ple find their best friend or soul mate through Buying Nothing. We couldn't possibly make all of these stories up, and there are too many to recount here. We are inundated with stories and confes-sions of true joy in finding dear friends through giving, asking, and gratitude. These are not just buddies, but the kind of people who are there for you for the milestones of your life. Each of the follow-ing is a real example of precious friends and soul mates who have been found through the simple revolutionary call to Buy Nothing:

- Officiants for intimate weddings.
- Friends who throw baby showers.
- The people who come to hold your hand while you wait out-side the emergency room for news about your child.
- The kind souls who clothe you and feed you when your house burns down.
- The friend who shows up to take care of your toddler when you're giving birth to your second baby.
- The best friend you call when you lose a loved one.

- Those with whom you spend your vacations.
- The official witness you want with you when you elope.
- The person you eventually marry.

Your willingness to ask for what you need and then to also meet the giver in person could be the catalyst in your own love story. And while you're in the business of asking, offer a few more things to give away. It always helps to show that you're actively taking part in the network of givers and receivers that's there to support this way of life. The more you give, the more good, in many forms, will come back to you. This is how it works, and the sooner you take part in this way of thinking, the sooner you'll reap rewards. Then, when you truly need something, you'll be in great standing to receive. People will be falling over themselves to give to you.

> **The more you give, the more good, in many forms, will come back to you.**

We Invite You to Ask

You're ready to put *asking* into practice. We invite you to make three kinds of asks. Your first ask will be a thing that you want or need, something that's on your shopping list. Provide a little story with your ask, explaining why you want or need this item. It could be something as weird and wild as this post that was published in our own local Buy Nothing group by dog owner Jamie Bechtel Morrison: "Sooo, i can't believe i am writing this butttttt i need dead rats. we are training our Search and Rescue dog (Atlas—whom some of you have met on his coyote searches...) to identify rat habitat for a conservation program (island conservation—amazing work). if you have dead rats i have a dedicated dead rat freezer. my god i wish i were joking..."

Jamie's story got a huge response and gave context for her strange ask, but also sparked a good conversation among community members about nontoxic rat control. Everyone was able to relate to that, as we have a big rat problem on Bainbridge Island, and Jamie was easily able to find six rats, given to her freely for training her dog. Win-win.

Your second ask will be for help, whether it's help with a project or repairing something. Think about what you need help with, write down the first things that come to mind, and then just put it out there! Maybe you need help assembling a piece of furniture that's been sitting in a box, or perhaps you need someone with a truck to help you move that old dryer out of your basement, or someone to come over and capture an enormous spider building a web in your house. Liesl once needed help translating a contract for work that was written in Japanese. Incredibly, a native Japanese speaker in our neighborhood was able to translate the one-page document with ease. It was a big ask in Liesl's mind, but an easy task for our neighbor.

The top three things on our all-time go-to list of what we always need help with would be (1) help deep cleaning the house, (2) help weeding an overgrown garden, and (3) finding a backup person to pick the kids up from an after-school event when we're tied up with a work obligation.

Your third ask will be something that's just for you. Was your first ask something for someone else in your family? We thought so. Now it's time to really do some thinking about what *you* want, something that you've considered getting but never did, that thing that will make you happy, that's not also for your children, grand-children, or your partner to enjoy. This needs to be something that you'd maybe call frivolous, or have thought about getting but never did because, well, it feels selfish to get things just for you. Go for it, and ask for what's on your secret wish list and see what happens. You might just get what you ask for.

Once you've figured out what you'd like to ask for, decide how you'd like to ask for them. You can ask within a large group of people, or you can make your request to a select few. The more people who witness your asking, the more you'll show them how to do it, too. Try all of the places you shared your first gives, the group of friends, family, neighbors, or coworkers you gave to in Step 1 to make your request for Step 2. Come to our buynothinggetevery thing.com discussion forum to talk about the challenges you feel in asking, and see how others might help you to overcome them. Feel free to blame your weird out-of-the-blue asks on this book. Confess to your friends and neighbors that you're undertaking this seven-step Buy Nothing challenge, your very own Buy Nothing, Get Everything plan, and perhaps they'll join you.

If you're feeling nervous, please take this to heart: we know the vulnerability that comes with asking for things can feel intimidating, but we are here as living proof that it's not only possible to survive it, it's key to building a thriving gift economy that will bring you what you want and need, not just in terms of stuff but also in a wealth of connections and joy.

STEP 3: REUSE & REFUSE

The three Rs slogan —"Reduce, Reuse, Recycle"—was introduced during the peak of the environmental movement in the 1970s, and the Rs are purposely arranged in order of greatest impact to least, which also happens to be in order from what seems hardest to easiest. Many of us are used to sorting our recyclables into a separate bin, and municipal pickup programs make it easy to get these items to those ready to transform them back into useful objects. Reuse is a little more demanding, but clearly better for the environment. Reducing can seem most difficult at first, since it challenges us to push back on our consumer culture and mind-set.

We believe it's high time to focus on the R that was left out, the one with the biggest immediate impact: Refuse. We want you to imagine a "buyerarchy": first Refuse, then Reduce, Reuse, and Recycle. When you *Refuse* to buy that brand-new, just-manufactured item in the first place, it will never take up nonrenewable resources or end up in our watersheds or landfills. Is there a way that you can avoid purchasing that item new? We love that the word *refuse* has two meanings: One is a noun (pronounced "ref-yüs")—the trash we discard into our garbage cans. The other is a verb (pronounced "rē-fyuze")—indicating an unwillingness to accept or grant something, literally saying no. In Buy Nothing–speak, the connection between the two words, depending on how you pronounce them, is enlightening. It's a reminder that if you "rē-fyuze" new purchases and "yuze" other people's things instead (by acquiring or borrowing them), there's a good chance you're reducing greenhouse gas emissions and the amount of "ref-yūs" headed to the landfill. In the waste hierarchy, when it comes to impacts on the environment, Reducing is up at the tippy top of the pyramid, with Recycling further down because it requires energy and produces waste. But prevention, or *Refusing*, clearly belongs at the pinnacle.

If these ideas sound like a throwback to bygone days, you're not off base. Buying Nothing is reminiscent of an era when Americans were urged to practice more frugal ways. During World War II the government asked citizens to "Use it up . . . wear it out . . . make it do . . . or do without," as seen in a United States war message prepared by the War Advertising Council and approved by the Office of War Information. Some environmentalists and scientists are sounding a similar alarm about resource recovery today to combat climate change and pollution. Many of us have relatives, like Rebecca's Grandma Inge, who lived through the war and passed on their frugal ways.

A NOTE FROM REBECCA:
GRANDMA INGE'S BUY NOTHING STORY

My Grandma Inge's path to survival during the Holocaust zigzagged from her family home in Danzig to England, to Danzig, to Berlin, to England, onto a ship that sank, back to England, then onto another ship that made it to Canada. With the help of strangers, she made her way to San Francisco, where she settled and became an artist and poet. She took pride in finding new uses for objects, and when my first daughter was born on the first night of Hanukkah, she told me how she had celebrated this holiday during the war. She'd had no candles, let alone a metal menorah to hold them, so she stuck wooden matches into a long crack in the surface of her table and let their quick light brighten her room for a few seconds each night. Reuse, repurposing, and foraging kept her alive in body and spirit during her refugee existence, and when she was resettled safely, she kept these habits and applied them to her art. Every day, she checked the ground as she walked, searching for anything she could use in a sculpture, painting, or collage. My sisters and I watched the ground for her and offered our found objects to her. She was delighted when I found an old-fashioned wristwatch that had been crushed by a car tire; she salvaged each tiny gear from its carcass for one of her multimedia works.

She crocheted odd bits of yarn into strange and wonderful animals that crinkled because she stuffed them with washed-clean plastic produce bags. During one summer family camping expedition, Grandma Inge bought me a pack of gum and turned each foil wrapper into a different wild animal, an entire circus to play with as we bumped along the coast of California in her motorhome. To this day I rely on her memory as my guide to reuse, and I think she'd be happy with the Buy Nothing movement.

How things have changed. For those of us who grew up in the 1980s, '90s, and early 2000s, where our popular culture encourages us to judge ourselves and others on the quantity, newness, and brand name of our possessions, a lifestyle of reuse-by-choice can seem, well, a bit uncool. So let us try to change your mind and perhaps help us all embrace Grandma Inge's spirit of creativity when it comes to making the old and discarded new again. Here are a few reasons why Reusing can have a positive impact:

- **Economic.** According to an analysis by the Institute for Local Self-Reliance, for each ten thousand tons of waste handled in a year, reuse creates from 28 jobs (wooden pallet repair for example) to 296 jobs (computer reuse). Landfills and incinerators create 1 job for each ten thousand tons of annual waste.[1]

- **Environmental.** Reuse trumps Recycling here. Recycling, or the transformation of a product at the end of its useful life into something new, requires the input of energy, both to transport the waste en masse to manufacturing facilities and to complete the actual breaking down and remaking of the material. Some materials have a closed-loop cycle, but many require the input of additional virgin material in order to be useful as consumer goods once again. Reuse can be done by individuals at home and by small local businesses, lowering energy input and transportation carbon footprints.

- **Personal.** Reuse sparks creative thinking and gives you great pride in your work as you turn old stuff into something repurposed and useful. Granted, we don't have stats on how much happier you'll be if you Reuse more often, but we've seen how this mentality has sparked surprising joy in Buy Nothing members time and again. Sarah in Connecticut loves showing off the secondhand mirror she repainted for a rustic chic look in her guest room. Storm Furness of Queensland, Australia, offers this lightbulb moment: If you've forgotten your shopping bag, help yourself to what you need from the store's plastic bag recycling bin, which is usually by the front door. And our own neighbor Michelle White places the base of hearts she has left over from romaine lettuce heads in a glass of water. They root and produce more lettuce right there on her windowsill. A reused lettuce heart, celery heart, and even green onions and beets can produce more food over time. Reuse takes many forms, and gives you the opportunity to look at your stuff in an entirely new way, bringing immense satisfaction when you've found ways to keep money in your wallet by finding new uses for what you already have.

Many people believe that Reuse takes time, and for those who work full-time, have kids, and live busy lives, Reuse just doesn't feel possible as it could require more work. We believe that Reuse can often be a shortcut, saving you a trip to the store or hours spent online sourcing something new. Learning how to replace things we typically buy—like single-use items, with more-durable reusable items we already have—could be the single most important step you take in Buying Nothing.

An Experiment in Buying Nothing

A few years ago, Rebecca took things to the next level and challenged herself to wear a single secondhand black cotton wrap sundress each day for a year, with every other bit of her wardrobe coming for free from the gift economy she was a part of. The clothing industry is the second-biggest polluter in the world behind the oil industry. We're buying more clothing and wearing it for shorter amounts of time. The EPA estimates that of the 16 million tons of textiles produced in 2015, 10.5 million of them were sent to landfills. Only 2.5 million tons were recycled, a number we can easily improve on since almost all textiles can be reused or recycled.[2] And while synthetic fabrics will never truly decompose, natural fibers can eventually be composted.

REBECCA'S ONE-DRESS EXPERIMENT

I wanted to find out: Could I really wear a single secondhand dress every single day, for an entire year? Would it hold up through all of my activities and regular washing? Would anyone around me notice? Would I get bored or find it impractical to have just one dress? I got answers to all of my questions: Yes, if you're careful about washing gently and air-drying, even a secondhand thin cotton sundress will last for a full year of daily wear. No, you will not break any unspoken social rules by wearing the same thing every day, especially with the addition of accessories that bring daily changes of color, texture, and pattern into your look. Truly, the only people who noticed were those I told; if I hadn't mentioned it, people were genuinely shocked to learn I'd been wearing the same dress every single day. I took away one big lesson from this surprise: people we work with every day pay less attention to the base of our wardrobe and much more to whatever is most colorful or visually exciting, which made it possible for me to enjoy a year of workdays, a wedding, a memorial service, holidays, hiking, and a school camping trip all in this one dress.

We don't expect many people to willingly replace their wardrobes with a single piece of clothing the way Rebecca did, but what she learned translates to all of us: we can build a personal style that rests on a very simple foundation, and those pieces do not need to be brand-new. Focus on the things you truly love and wear the heck out of them.

Why Shopping Feels Good and Buying Nothing Can Feel Better

We know the allure of new purchases: the fresh energy that item holds; the idea that you have something new that belongs just to you; the accomplishment one feels when we're finally able to afford something we've saved up for; or when a purchase signifies a milestone reached, like your first business suit. We're not suggesting you cut these experiences and the positive feelings they bring out of your life completely. We want to show you how to find the same joy, and some new pleasures, by Buying Nothing instead of buying new.

Many of us know the quick pleasure and ease of online shopping for everything from books to bathing suits to boxed-up mattresses. We are all wired to get an immediate dopamine hit (a neurotransmitter released by brain cells, with the reputation as "the feel-good hormone") when we anticipate getting what we want at the push of one button. When the product is delivered to our front door two days later, we get another dopamine hit from that delayed gratification. Our newest shoppers, Generation Z, the under-twenty-two-year-old demographic, are greatly influenced to buy clothing and everything else they want through their social media platforms (we know this firsthand as mothers of teens). We get it, the thrill of the new possession is very real. But this same dopamine hit is available to each of us when we receive what we want and need, from the mundane and necessary to the longed-for luxuries and treasures, free of charge, gifted from our community.

We have seen over and over again that when people choose to share and Reuse things, these actions bring at least as much joy as buying them new ever could. Yes, humans are wired to gather stuff and store it for times when resources are scarce. But we're also wired to feel joy in connecting with our fellow humans and to share resources, ensuring our mutual survival and success as a society.

Reuse is one of the most important steps for Buying Nothing, and also one of the most easily misunderstood. We get that the thought of Reusing can trigger memories of relatives who lived through war and want and who brought their survival habits into peacetime as well, like the way your grandmother refused to toss her broken floral couch from the seventies. But Reuse can feel very different in a gift economy mind-set, because there is an incentive to share instead of hoard, to give and receive to fit the immediate needs of your home. When we let go of that survival-mode mentality, Reuse can save us time, money, and mental energy.

As a start, try assessing each new item that enters your home with an eye toward its next use. Take pasta sauce, for instance: pick one in a glass jar with a wide mouth, so you can use that jar first to store leftovers (no need to rinse, just put your saucy pasta right back in there and pack it for lunch the next day), then for any one of a thousand household storage uses in the future, and finally to hold flowers for a friend when you have too many jars and need to make space. This attitude works with everything you want or need. Clothing, for example, can be cut into rags to replace paper towels. Liesl became a convert when all she had to clean up a cat's hair ball accident was an old T-shirt; eight years later, she still hasn't needed to buy new paper towels thanks to a steady supply of worn-out kids' shirts that can be washed and reused or used to suppress weeds in the garden when the job is just too messy to touch that rag again.

When you must buy food in plastic packaging (which, let's be honest, is pretty inevitable), think up creative ways to Reuse it. We've found a local flour tortilla brand that comes in very sturdy plastic slide-lock bags, which means we get all the quesadillas our kids want to eat as well as bags that stand up to years of Reuse for bulk food purchases, frozen meals, school lunches, travel packing, wet hiking socks, and all of the other things that want a water-proof covering. Creatively Reusing everyday items will save you time, space, and money, and give you a sense of pride in your own ingenuity and resourcefulness.

Once you've mastered Reusing, you can move on to other Rs, like renovating, reupholstering, refurbishing, restoring, remodel-ing, repainting, and repairing. Furniture, lamps, and mirrors are a great example. You can find these around your home or get them through the gift economy, then refurbish them to make them uniquely yours. Making what's old into something customized and new for you is immensely gratifying.

The next time you need something, look at what you already own before you go looking online or in a store. For example, when you realize you don't have any shorts to wear, but you do have some holey jeans, you can make some cute cutoff shorts with them, your new favorite pair of shorts. Or maybe you'll discover a long-forgotten pair buried deep in your closet during a Give clean-out. Don't have anything to repurpose? Ask for what you need in your gift economy—Reuse can include other people's things, not just your own. These kinds of small revelations show how life without buying more stuff isn't all that different. We think of this as embracing the wise and nonwasteful way our ancestors lived, fast-forwarding the best of their practices into our twenty-first-century homes.

Life Less Groceries

One way to save money and resources is in the kitchen. Most of us tend to overbuy at the supermarket, and then we're left with waste when the produce goes bad. The USDA and EPA estimate that each person in the United States disposed of 218.9 pounds of wasted food in 2010 alone, and are working together to halve that amount by 2030.[3] We think we can each reach beyond that goal more quickly with a Buy Nothing way of life.

Stock your shelves with basic ingredients and favorite herbs and spices, then use up what's in your larder, rather than buying specialty ingredients for fancy new recipes. You don't have to buy foods that you only need a bit of and that will likely sit around and take up space until you find another recipe for them. Stock up on your favorite basics and cook with those, and not only will you save space on your shelves and save waste from un-eaten ingredients, but you'll save your money, too. When you have leftovers that won't be eaten imminently, stash them in the freezer. You'll be happy to reheat them on a night you don't want to cook.

10 THINGS TO REUSE INSTEAD OF TOSS

Here's a quick list of ten common things to Reuse instead of toss, to help stretch your meals and groceries further and reduce your shopping bills:

1. *Citrus Peels.* We use them as ingredients for a great all-purpose cleaner (recipe on page 100), for orange or lemon zest, dried out as fire starters, or thrown into the bottoms of garbage cans since they're great deodorizers.
2. *Broccoli, Cauliflower, Swiss Chard.* Don't throw out the stems. We put the chopped stems in stir-fry and salads or turn them into fridge pickles in a jar of vinegar with a clove of garlic and a dash of honey.
3. *Coffee Grounds.* You can use coffee grounds as an exfoli-ant for your face, feet, arms, or legs or, in a pinch, to scrub your dishes. We save money on fertilizer for our blueberry bushes and sprinkle coffee grounds at their base instead. Blueberries love them! And we've also been known to use coffee grounds in steak marinades and as a secret ingre-dient in brownies (very fine espresso grounds work best for this).

4. *Eggshells.* Put a handful of clean crushed white eggshells into a fine mesh bag, throw them in with your whites in the laundry, and the shells will help take the gray out of your light-colored fabrics. No need for bleach! Or use the shells as your natural calcium supplement. Research has shown that eggshells have many beneficial properties.[4] Skip the pills and simply bake your eggshells at 350 degrees Fahrenheit for eight minutes. Let them cool and then grind them to a fine powder. Add your supplement (a teaspoon or less) to your favorite smoothie or juice once a day. Check with your health-care provider to discuss safety and appropriate dosage.

5. *Wine Corks.* Wine corks make for great . . . wait for it . . . corkboards! Use an old picture frame or mirror and glue the corks into place, fully covering the mirror or backing of your frame. Did you know that *cork* is both a noun and a verb? Use your corks to . . . you guessed it . . . cork all kinds of liquids in pretty reusable glass bottles. Search online for "cork reuse" and you'll find hundreds of other ideas. Lastly, our favorite: cork pot lid grippers. If you have metal pot lids that get hot to the touch, squeeze two or three corks under the lid handle, perpendicular to it, so you touch these instead of the hot metal. Presto! Cool to the touch even after hours of cooking.

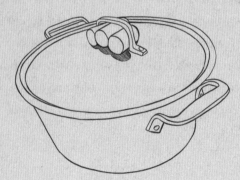

6. ***Onion Skins.*** Throw them in soups and slow cookers: More than five hundred thousand tons of onion waste is thrown out each year in the European Union alone, and this bulb, including all the fiber in its skin, is nutritious![5]

7. ***Parmesan Rinds.*** Save them and throw them into your soup stock. They'll liven up your minestrone or vegetable soup!

8. ***Bean Water.*** If you cook beans in a pressure or slow cooker, save your bean water; it makes a delicious and nutritious base for soups.

9. ***Tea Leaves.*** Dry used black tea is a stink remover. Tea leaves make a great deodorizer to remove odors from your fridge, carpet, and dog bed. Herbal and black tea leaves make great instant compost for potted plants or outdoor gardens.

10. ***Toothbrushes.*** Don't toss those used toothbrushes. They make for great cleaning tools. Keep one under the sink for scrubbing around faucets and sink edges. Label another one for use as a fingernail cleaner after gardening. Store one in your cleaning supplies bucket for spot cleaning carpets and furniture. And save one for the laundry room for scrubbing out stains.

We plan our meals around the vegetables that are in season in our gardens and nearby farms and use up what's in the fridge and pantry to augment those main-course veggies or fruits. When blackberries are in season, we pick all we can for free in local parks and freeze them so we can have blackberry smoothies for breakfast all year long. And kale, which grows twelve months in our gardens in the Pacific Northwest, is a staple that can be used in anything from smoothies, to salads, to snacks (many kale haters love kale chips), to main-course veggie sautés.

Before you shop, make a list of core ingredients that will work in a variety of dishes during the week, to avoid impulse buying. We've found that whole foods are the simplest, most affordable, and healthiest staples for our meals, and the fewer ingredients in the meal, the quicker it comes together. The staple ingredients we buy (usually in bulk) at the store are sweet potatoes, almonds, cashews, peanut butter, dried black and pinto beans, dried chickpeas and lentils, flour and corn tortillas, rice, flour, and pasta. From these ingredients, we can make hundreds of different meals. Three-ingredient meals are also a great way to save food, money, and time. Just do a search online and you'll be amazed by what you can find. Some of our favorites are cheddar-broccoli-egg muffins, banana-almond-egg pancakes, banana-berry smoothies, peanut butter bars, and garlic-kale fried eggs.

FORAGE INSTEAD OF BUYING

Imagine being able to cook a week's worth of meals for a family of four from two bags of groceries or less. This is what we aim to do, and we're successful because when we have the time we forage for and grow many of the main ingredients we use, like nettles (when in season); watercress (growing wild); berries (we pick and freeze); garden greens like kale and collards; potatoes, onions, and garlic that we grow and store; mushrooms (foraged), and our hens' eggs. Fallingfruit.org is a great worldwide resource for finding foods to forage anywhere on Earth. Wherever you live, rural, suburban, or urban, Falling Fruit can direct you to the abundance growing all around you. When you're new to foraging, follow the golden rule: never eat anything you can't positively identify. If you're unfamiliar with your local fruits, mushrooms, nuts, and plants, ask a local expert to give you the gift of guidance.

LIESL'S 5-MEALS-IN-1 CHICKEN

In Liesl's house, chicken is one of her family's favorite sources of protein, and they use up the whole chicken. Here are tips on how to get five meals out of one chicken. "We start with the whole raw chicken, usually roasting it through Mark Bittman's *New York Times* recipe.[6] Then we eat many meals from it, starting with Meal 1: a dinner of roasted sliced chicken breast, drumsticks, thighs, and wings. Meal 2: enchiladas or stir-fry or fried rice, using the remaining bits of meat. Meal 3: we use the bones as a base for chicken stock, along with vegetable scraps like saved onion skins, garlic skins, and carrot ends. You can freeze the bones if you don't plan to make the stock right away. Meal 4: we save the stock and reserve the bones, setting the stock aside for other uses, then add more water to the bones and do a long slow simmer of them until we've made a bone broth and the bones are soft. Meal 5: at which point we finally turn those soft bones into dog food by throwing them into a very-high-powered blender with a little bone broth and grind it all down to a paste with no shards present. We store it in the fridge in a mason jar to add to our pup's meals. By the time we're done with it, that chicken has fed everyone in the family and nothing remains."

Step 3: Reuse & Refuse

Other than using up what we have in the larder and the garden for our weekly meals, what else can we Refuse to buy? Here are some stress-free ways to say no to single-use disposables (SUDs) and yes to more-durable and -sustainable alternatives.

To reduce your waste on the go, carry a reusable mug with you so that you don't waste disposable coffee cups (bonus, you get a discount at some coffee shops when you bring your own!); keep a set of flatware (bamboo ware is lightweight) in your purse or at your office so you don't have to use plastic utensils; and bring a foldable, reusable cloth bag with you at all times so you can carry your groceries home in it (or keep bags in the trunk of your car).

Please don't feel pressured to do *all* of the things we share below. Our lists and ideas are meant to inspire you to Reuse and Recycle more, not stress out. Choose the suggestions that feel good and inspiring for you. Take the easiest steps for you first, and then challenge yourself to delve deeper later. Channeling our grandmothers' frugal ways, here's our list of fifty items we no longer scribble onto our shopping lists:

50 Things We Never Buy

1. **Paper Towels.** TreeHugger tells us that disposable paper products make up one-fourth of our landfill waste, and we've learned from trusty statistics that it would take fifty-one thousand trees per day to replace the number of paper towels that are tossed each day.[7] So use cloth "towels" instead! They don't have to be fancy. You can use your rags or make cloth wipes from old kitchen towels, holey sheets,

even old T-shirts. If you keep your cloth wipes in a pretty basket or drawer in your kitchen, they'll be close at hand for all cleanup purposes. Throw them in the washing machine, and you've got reusable wiping towels for every gooky mess you can think of.

2. **Paper Napkins.** Use your cloth ones and Reuse them again and again. If you don't have pretty cloth napkins, consider making your own by repurposing old cotton sheets, a shirt, skirt, or tablecloth. We both have about thirty cotton napkins stored at all times in a drawer, ready for everyday use. Napkins are very easy to make: just search for "how to make cloth napkins" on the internet, and you'll see lots of great ideas.

3. **Tissues.** Use a hanky! Your grandpa did.

4. **Garbage Bags.** Yup, we don't buy them anymore because there's really no need to line our garbage bins if it's all thrown into a deep container at the transfer station. Depending upon your municipality, you may not need to line your bins with plastic that's just headed to the landfill anyway. Look into it, and thank us later. If you must have your garbage in bags, Reuse pet food bags, feed sacks, or any other large bags that you or your giving network have in excess, rather than contributing more new polyethylene to the landfill. Remember, you can ask for what you need. Your asking will enable another to give, and they may be thrilled to give you what they were otherwise going to have to pay to trash.

5. **Resealable Bags.** Zip-top and slide-lock plastic bags are useful in so many ways. Reusing them, rather than buying them, will save you a bundle. Just turn them inside out and wash them in your kitchen sink with cool water and dish

soap—since they're made of polyethylene, which is imper-meable plastic, you can wash them just as you'd wash your dishes. We then place them on a wooden bag dryer that is a staple by the kitchen sink, but you can make a bag dryer by putting chopsticks in a toothbrush holder cup and plac-ing the bags upside down to dry over the chopsticks. Easy. Some people dry the bags on their refrigerator, sticking them to the door with their fridge magnets. We take this one step further, and actually wash all kinds of plastic bags for Reuse. Hopefully this book has encouraged you to never buy a plastic bag again, and to use more environmentally sound materials like glass jars to store food. But if you need plastic bags, washing and Reusing them is a great way to go. And when they've reached the end of their useful life, recycle them! Resealable bags can be thrown in your plas-tic bag recycling bin at the supermarket, so long as they're clean and dry.

6. **Freezer Bags.** In our opinion, freezer bags are just another marketing scam. Simply use two reusable resealable bags instead, to have thicker insulation between your frozen food and the inside of your freezer. (See #5 for washing out the resealable bags and then using them again.) If you buy frozen food that comes in thick resealable bags, by all means, Reuse them.

7. **Reusable Cloth Bags.** These are the bags you bring with you to go shopping so you don't have to use a store's "paper or plastic." Stash them along with your reusable mug and utensils. Rebecca's no-sew T-shirt bag takes ten minutes or less to make and is a simple alternative to the plastic and paper bags found in stores.

REBECCA'S NO-SEW T-SHIRT BAG

By repurposing a used T-shirt and cutting down on single-use bags, this T-shirt bag is a Buy Nothing win-win.

- Cut off the sleeves of an old T-shirt to make the outside edges of the bag's handles. You can turn these into rags; these are especially good for drying glasses, both the kind you read with and the kind you drink from.

- Cut off the neckline to form the bag's opening and the inside edges of the handles. Set the neckline loop aside for another use—I love to use these around my journals, as head or hair bands, and to tie up my tomato plants in the summer.

- Does your T-shirt have a turned-over and stitched hem at its waist? If so, you can cut it off and save it with the neckline to make this next step easier.

- Fold the shirt flat on a table and take the right and left corners of the bottom in hand. Tie them together in a square knot (right over left, then left over right) to form a closed bottom for your bag. If they're too short to tie, use that neckline loop to gather and tie them together on the inside or outside of the shirt (either works, pick the look you like best). Your bag is ready to use.

8. **All-Purpose Citrus Cleaner.** Use citrus peels and vinegar to create an all-purpose cleaner. Just throw your orange (or lemon or lime) peels in a large jar, and add distilled white vinegar to cover the peels. Add more peels over time until the jar is full, making sure the vinegar covers all your peels. Let the jar of citrus peels sit for at least a month and you'll have an excellent citrus cleaner that'll cut through grease just like any store-bought cleaner. We put a mixture of one part orange peel vinegar to two parts water in a spray bottle, and we're good to clean! If you don't love the vinegar smell, you can cut it with your favorite essential oil to make it the perfect scent for your home.

9. **Laundry Detergent.** We've both used the following concentrated laundry detergent powder recipe, off and on, for years. You'll find many variations of this recipe online. They all work well. A full load in a top-loading washing machine needs only one tablespoon (maybe a scant two tablespoons if things are horribly soiled). A single batch of this lasts a couple of months for a three-person household.

    What you'll need: borax, washing soda, and a bar of soap (*nothing* beats a bar of Fels-Naptha for stain fighting). What to do: Use the fine-shred side of a hand grater to grate your bar of soap into a large mixing bowl, or chop the bar into one-inch chunks, and then use a food processor to chop it to fine pieces. Add 1 cup each of borax and washing soda. Mix by hand wearing protective, reusable rubber gloves. You can also use a food processor as long as you chop the soap into small chunks to protect your blade, and wash it very well once your batch is finished. Blend until everything is well blended and mostly smooth, with the curls of the grated soap broken down. Store the finished mix in a large jar and keep the lid screwed on tight between uses. Keep this clearly labeled mixture out of the reach of children and anyone else who might ingest it, as these ingredients are not safe for consumption! You can add white vinegar to your loads as a fabric softener to reduce soap buildup on the clothing and your washer. All of the ingredients are readily available in recyclable plastic-free packaging, and for less than what the same amount of commercially made laundry detergent generally costs.

10. **Dryer Sheets or Laundry Softener.** Make dryer balls instead! These will reduce your dryer time by at least 10 percent. They also are a replacement for fabric softener and dryer sheets as they remove static cling, soften your fabrics, and can even add a lovely scent if you opt to use essential oils on the balls. To make them, all you need is an old wool sweater or 100 percent wool yarn. Gather your sweater (or yarn) into a ball and use some extra wool yarn to wind around it, tightening it into a sphere the size of a large orange. Now, grab a few oddball socks out of your single socks box (we're sure you have plenty) and place one wool ball inside one sock and tie off the end. Wool felts easily when combined with water, heat, and agitation. Throw your sock balls into your washing machine with the cycle on high, in hot water (and add a dash of detergent and a few towels or T-shirts to fill up the load). You can wash them in a hot cycle twice just to be sure that the wool balls are felting up. If you don't have easy access to a washing machine, you can use a large tub of hot soapy water set in your bathtub or out on the ground along with an old-fashioned washboard

to agitate and rub the wool into balls. Then toss them into the dryer and put them on high heat until dry. Now untie the socks and release the felted wool balls from their sock enclosures. They should have felted up pretty nicely. You can put a few drops of your favorite essential oil on the wool balls about every fourth load you dry to give your laundry a nice scent.

11. **Oven Cleaner.** Remember that all-purpose citrus cleaner we told you about in #8? Mix a solution of fifty-fifty all-purpose citrus cleaner and water, and use it in your oven. It should cut through any grease or char without the chemical fumes of conventional cleaner.

12. **Carpet Cleaner.** Sprinkle a light layer of baking soda mixed with a few drops of your favorite essential oil on your carpet, and then vacuum it up. This freshens the carpet. If you add borax to the mixture, it will clean the carpet. Be careful if you have pets and children, though, as borax can be a mild irritant and isn't safe to ingest.

13. **Window-Washing Liquid.** Use one part white vinegar and two parts water with a small drop of dish soap to clean your windows, and wipe them down with newspaper instead of paper towels, which just leave lint residue on your glass.

14. **Dish-Scouring Powder.** Use this concoction when you have stubborn cooked food stuck to dishes, pots, and cast iron. We like ten drops each of tea tree and lavender oil (or oil of your choosing) in enough baking soda to fill a twenty-four-ounce reused marinara sauce jar. Yes, that's it. It seems diabolically simple, but really it's heavenly. It works! It smells wonderful since you use oils *you* like. Punch a few holes into the lid of your jar, sprinkle the baking soda on wet dishes in the sink, then scrub by hand or with one of

our DIY pot scrubbers (see #15), and both your dishes and sink will be sparkling clean. Worried about sanitation? The majority of dish soap does not disinfect dishes. It does remove food particles that can provide fuel and safe harbor for harmful bacteria, and it cleans the surface of dishes to remove oils and other substances we don't want to touch or eat again. This combination of baking soda and essential oils does all of this, and when you use your fingers instead of a sponge, you cut out another common vector for bacteria. Still worried? Add a few drops of your favorite soap.

15. **Pot Scrubbers.** Old, used aluminum foil works really well as a pot scrubber for at least a week if you crumple it up. Don't laugh. It works, and when your crumpled foil gets all flat, just throw it in your recycle bin (if your city takes foil) and use your next piece of dirty aluminum foil as a scrubber. You can also save your produce bags made of stiff plastic netting, the kind of bags that citrus fruits and potatoes are commonly packed in, and transform them into scrubbers: Gather your stiff netting bags and accordion fold them into segments two to three inches long. Tie the center as tightly as you can with a length of string. Once the bundle is securely knotted, clip the ends of the string (cotton remnants can be composted) and then cut each loop of bag to fluff the ends up.

16. **Swiffer Pads.** If you use a Swiffer-style mop, you don't have to buy those pads over and over again. Just use a washcloth, microfiber cloth, or cloth diaper, wash, and Reuse.

17. **Bottled Water.** Unless you're putting together your emergency preparedness kit, let's just skip buying bottled water when we're thirsty. Please? And while we're at it, how about

forgoing plastic-bottled beverages in general? The third most prolific item found washed up on our shorelines is ... plastic bottles. And what do you think number four is? Plastic bottle caps![8] This is going to require a little work on your part, but if you're away from home, you can bring a stainless steel or glass water bottle with you wherever you go, and refill it with water to quench your thirst. This works just as well for fancier drinks—add some flavor to your water with a slice of fresh lemon or a handful of mint leaves, pour home-brewed iced tea into your bottle, or fill it with your other favorite drink from home. Fifty billion plastic water bottles are discarded each year in the US alone, and now we know a large percentage ends up in our oceans. If you use a reusable water bottle instead, that's about 156 plastic water bottles you could prevent from ending up in our waste streams, and possibly even our oceans, each year.[9]

KICK YOUR CONVENIENCE STORE SINGLE-USE BEVERAGE FIX

Occasionally, our families walk the mile to our neighborhood store. We tend to bring bags to collect the roadside trash. Each time, we pick up more than fifty beverage containers. In 2009, Keep America Beautiful conducted a study of 240 roadways across the country and determined that there are approximately 6,729 pieces of litter per mile of roadway in the United States.[10] The study also found that 53 percent of the roadside litter comes from motorists, and roads near a convenience store tended to have 11 percent more litter, with 40–60 percent of that roadside waste coming from beverage containers. The Environmental Working Group published a study that claims, "Every 27 hours Americans consume enough bottled water to circle the entire equator with plastic bottles stacked end to end."[11]

Not all of us are lucky enough to have safe drinking water in our homes.[12] If you rely on bottled water you will save money and create less plastic waste when you buy it in gallon jugs or larger and use them to fill a reusable water bottle that will help you to kick the single-use beverage habit. When you discover the amount of energy, toxins, and virgin materials needed to produce that single serving bottle or can, you might reconsider the need for it. Use your own bottle and fill 'er up. If your water supply at home is safe, offer jugs of it to your neighbors who may need it.

18. **Cling Wrap.** This thin plastic film polymer that's sticky enough to cling to itself and just about everything else it touches can't be recycled. Store leftovers in glass jars whenever you can, or use a plate to cover a bowl, or, in a pinch, use reusable aluminum foil. Rebecca has a great method for making her own beeswax cloth wrap (look for it on page 160), which acts a little like cling wrap, if you need to cover your food in the fridge or elsewhere.

PVC—NOT FOR ME

Beyond the environmental concerns, there are health reasons to give up plastics. There is emerging evidence of a correlation between exposure to phthalates in plastics and lower male fertility.[13] High exposure to phthalates (in workers using PVC flooring, for example) is associated with low testosterone levels, which has a cascade of ill effects on male bodies. We are learning quickly that the male reproductive tract is particularly sensitive to phthalate exposure, in ways that impact future generations as well as the men exposed now.

19. **Notepaper.** Notes can be written down on any scrap paper. Next time you're going through your mail, hold on to the junk mail and letters that are single sided. Use the back side for notes and as draft paper in your printer. We can generally go a year without buying notepaper this way! You can also use envelopes, paper grocery bags too worn for carrying, or anything with room for a few paragraphs, a list, or some doodles.

20. **Padded Envelopes and Mailers.** We receive so many of these throughout the year that we save them, Reuse them, and also give them away to neighbors who have small businesses and need envelopes for mailings. Just cover over the address with a nice address label and it looks professional enough. Sometimes we bring attention to the fact that they're reused padded envelopes by writing "Please reuse this envelope" on the back. Most people will appreciate that their mailer was used once before. Padded mailers also make excellent padding for fragile items when packing for a move. Use them just as you would use bubble wrap.

21. **Wrapping Paper and Ribbons.** There are so many wonderful alternatives to wrapping paper, including cloth, paper bags, newspaper, your children's artwork, and old maps or

book pages. We have a stash of reusable cloth bags that we make each year to use as gift bags. And we save wrapping paper and paper gift bags, too, Reusing them, of course. Simply look on any shoreline and you'll find ribbons there from helium birthday balloons set free. They don't decompose. To keep ribbons off our beaches, Reuse the ribbons that arrive on gifts you receive, and create your own gift ribbons from strips of fabric, twine, and cords that find their way into your home.

22. **Birthday Cards, Greeting Cards, Valentines.** These are an original handmade art that has been usurped by Hallmark. Get out your scissors, some pretty paper, and some glue and get creative! With some old-fashioned literal cutting and pasting, you can turn things around the house—magazines, homemade art, found objects, stickers—into collaged greeting cards that your friends and family members will love to receive in the mail. Kid art is especially appreciated by grandparents, uncles, and aunts! Give yourself extra reuse credit if you find discarded cardstock from other projects or past cards to use as a base. This works year-round for love notes of all kinds.

23. **Gift Tags.** We've been known, over the holidays, to repurpose last year's cards as gift tags. You can do the same, of course, with all the pretty cards you receive throughout the year. Cut off the page where the nice note was written to you, and turn them into personalized tags to add to your gifts.

24. **Christmas Ornaments and Decorations.** Ornaments are one of the sweetest items to make as a family, as they're treasured year after year. In Liesl's household, it's a tra-

dition to hand make at least one ornament each for the tree. Just google "homemade ornaments" or look some up on Pinterest. They can be made from things you have in the house. Liesl's come from old DVDs/CDs, tin can lids, doll arms and legs (seriously, they look like candy canes if you paint sparkly candy stripes on them), pine cones, you name it.

25. **Pens.** Pens are everywhere, as it turns out—just look in every parking lot and on your sidewalks. The sad truth is that when we leave them out there, they get run over by cars and quickly become bits of microplastic, ready to be washed into the nearest storm drain. And on our island, where do you think those storm drains go? Directly into Puget Sound. Pick them up when you can and you might never have to buy (or borrow) a pen again!

THE FOURTH KINGDOM

It's no surprise that plastic is showing up in our environment, in particular our waters, in such alarming numbers. Ever spill a few packing peanuts from a box, or a plastic bag on a breezy day, to see them disperse rapidly in the wind? It's easy to understand why plastic is ubiquitous when we look closely at the genesis of the polymer itself, how it was designed to last, and why it's here to stay.

Plastic arrived on the planet when in 1907 Belgian émigré Leo Baekeland invented a material that he named after himself—"Bakelite," otherwise known as the thirty-six-letter megaword: polyoxybenzylmethylenglycolanhydride. It was the first man-made polymer, composed entirely of synthetic chemicals. He had produced a rigid yet formable plastic that was particularly suitable for the emerging electrical and automobile industries because of its extraordinarily high resistance to electricity, heat, and chemical action. Science had outdone the natural world. Plastic, from the Greek *plastikos*, meaning "moldable," was revolutionary. Our animals, minerals, and vegetables couldn't create anything quite as robust, the Bakelite Corporation later claimed to the media. They had created "a fourth kingdom, where boundaries are unlimited."[14] Today, that fourth kingdom is taking over our planet in a human-sanctioned invasion, silently wreaking havoc.

26. **Styrofoam Peanuts or Bubble Wrap.** Polystyrene in the form of packing peanuts is one of the ugliest things to find out in the environment, and it ends up there as readily as hair ties and ballpoint pens. In fact, polystyrene is one of the most common types of plastic pollution found in our natural world. We're not suggesting you run around chasing every packing peanut into the bushes. But you should never have to buy this stuff because most people are trying to get rid of it. Just ask for packing supplies and you'll make lots of friends. People *love* to off-load their packing peanuts.

27. **Cardboard Boxes.** People really do buy these. If there's one thing that we can guarantee that you can find out in the universe for free, it's a box. Don't buy boxes. Just ask for them. Liquor stores are particularly willing to get rid of their boxes. Some communities, like ours, even have on-

line groups for community members to get rid of or acquire boxes, and other supplies, for moving.

28. **String.** We never buy string anymore because we aren't ashamed to say we salvage it from all sorts of items like our chicken feed sacks. String is something you can easily ask for in your giving network, because chances are that your neighbors have a little stockpile, too.

29. **Rubber Bands.** They come on some pieces of produce like broccoli stems to hold them together (as if one might lose the other somehow). They come on newspapers. We find them (here it comes again, wait for it) on the streets. They're just littered all over the place. Bend down, and pick them up. That's all it takes to recover all the lost rubber bands in the world to put them back into circulation.

30. **Plastic Children's Toys.** Just ask any parent for them, and they'll gladly give you a box or three. This is one category of items we pledged to never buy when our kids were little. They didn't know any better and were happy to receive used but new-to-them toys. We're particularly passionate about this when it comes to those plastic beach toys. So many forgotten beach toys end up on our beaches—we'd love to see people simply stop buying them. Rebecca's family has used some great alternatives, like a collection of vintage aluminum and copper gelatin molds that spend the summers building sandcastles and the colder months hanging on her backyard fence as outdoor art. Old Bundt cake pans, metal baking measuring cups, bowls, and utensils all make wonderful tools for digging, building sandcastles, and collecting treasures at the beach.

31. **Plastic Straws.** Plastic straws are a scourge upon the land

(and water) with straws tallying as the seventh most preva-
lent item found on our coastlines. Plastic straws suck, and
they float, too. They will also never ever leave this planet,
but will break down into minuscule bits to be consumed by
our marine life. If you can, use your lips instead; if you're a
person who needs straws to drink, try one of the growing
number of alternatives to plastic. There are straws made
of glass, bamboo, metal, and even silicone. (Silicone, unlike
plastic, is a polymer produced from naturally occurring
silicon. Try one of the brands that is reusable and can even
be burned to a biodegradable ash at the end of its useful
life.)[15] Rebecca's giant fennel stalks, by the way, make excellent straws.

32. **Plastic Utensils.** We are so forked as a civilization: we see
a lot of plastic forks, knives, and spoons on our beaches,
washed up on the shoreline. A recent study found that plastic utensils were among the top ten kinds of plastic trash
found on shorelines in California.[16] If we all just used metal
or bamboo cutlery, we'd reduce this plastic scourge on our
planet quickly. Refuse plastic utensils. Bring a metal or
bamboo set with you in your backpack or purse, wherever
you go, and you'll have your to-go ware to help reduce plastic waste. Keep them in your car glove box for eating on the
go. We collect metal cutlery throughout the year, finding
it in free boxes around town, and then offer it up for use
at everything from classroom birthday parties to local fes-
tivals. Considering plastic utensils are one of the greatest
contributors to the nine million tons of plastic entering our
oceans each year, we think plastic disposables like utensils,
plastic bags, and straws should simply be outlawed.

SUDS

In her book *Plastic: A Toxic Love Story*, Susan Freinkel describes the quiet infiltration plastics have made into our lives: "In product after product, market after market, plastics challenged traditional materials and won, taking the place of steel in cars, paper and glass in packaging, and wood in furniture.... By 1979, production of plastics exceeded that of steel. In an astonishingly brief period, plastic had become the skeleton, the connective tissue, and the slippery skin of modern life."[17]

We've become addicted to plastic and the convenience it brings us. It's cheap, versatile, lightweight, durable, and resistant to corrosion. But no one thought about where it would all go. According to Freinkel, the average American in the 1960s consumed thirty pounds of plastic products, and by 2010 consumption had reached three hundred pounds, ringing in $300 billion in sales. Most of those plastics are made to be used only once and then thrown away. Those would become the scourge of our natural world, the single-use disposables, or SUDs, one of the most prevalent plastics we see in the environment today: straws, coffee cups, coffee lids, water bottles and caps, plastic cutlery, and candy wrappers. You get the picture.

33. **Paper or Plastic Disposable Plates.** You know where we're going with this. Use your everyday plates, um, every day and you'll never have to buy paper plates again. And acquiring a set of plates you don't really care about chipping or using for picnics or other events will save you from the temptation of buying paper plates for your picnics. People

prefer to eat on real plates, and there's no lack of them in the universe. So use them! We have enamel plates and bowls we camp with, and a gifted set of midcentury glass "hostess plates" that are perfect for outdoor free concerts and picnics all summer.

34. **Plastic Lighters.** Plastic "disposable" lighters replace matches way too often. Even though laws in some cities prohibit smoking, and lighting up is in steady decline these days, some bars and restaurants still put out free matchbooks for you to take home to use for your pyrotechnics. Matches, made of paperboard and wood, which are renewable resources, work just as well for all of our lighting needs, plastic-free.

35. **Vegetable Stock.** This one is so easy you'll be amazed that it has been hiding in plain sight for years. When you peel onions and garlic and cut off the ends of your zucchini or the insides of your bell peppers or have peelings from your potatoes, save those veggie scraps! Put them in a jar in the freezer and keep adding to them. Or throw them in a jar in your fridge that you add to every day. Then, once a week, put some water in a pot, pour your veg scraps in it, add some herbs and a pinch of salt if you feel so inclined, and let it boil, on low, for an hour or so. Strain out the vegetable scraps (put them in your compost), and you've got beautiful vegetable broth to use as a base for soups or other cooking. When we steam vegetables, we use the leftover veggie water as an excellent starter liquid for soups.

36. **Salad Dressings.** Remember the simple balsamic and olive oil dressing or a mustard vinaigrette? Just make your own delicious dressings in a jar! If you make them in bulk, you'll have spare dressing to last you a week or two. They

get better with age and will give you no excuse for not eating your greens. Try this quick faux Caesar dressing recipe and you won't be disappointed: Crush 4–6 cloves garlic, and place it in your favorite jar. Add 1 cup extra-virgin olive oil. Add about ¼ teaspoon fish sauce. (Yes, fish sauce. Be sure to buy it in a glass bottle.) Add about ½ cup freshly grated Parmesan cheese. Add 1–2 tablespoons red wine vinegar or homemade vinegar from your fruit scraps (which you'll learn how to do on page 149). Adjust the vinegar and fish sauce to taste, and done! Every time you use the dressing, you can add a little more cheese for added flavor. Our children just love this rich dressing.

37. **Taco Spice Blend, Italian Spice Blend, Other Seasoning Combos.** The store-bought mixes are generally not very healthy; they have way too much sodium and are filled with all sorts of additives. So make your own, and in bulk! It'll only take you a few minutes to make your own seasoning mix that will last through many meals. Here's Liesl's easy taco spice seasoning recipe (makes about 1⅔ cups). Add all of the ingredients below to a jar. Shake well to mix. Then store in a cool dark place:

- ½ cup chili powder (We both like pure ground-up chilies. Liesl sometimes uses chili powders she finds in Mexico; Rebecca finds hers in the grocery bulk spices. Go with your favorite!)
- ⅓ cup cumin
- 3 teaspoons garlic powder
- 3 teaspoons onion powder
- 1 tablespoon coarsely ground pepper

- 2–3 tablespoons ground coriander seeds
- 2 tablespoons paprika (sometimes we add smoked paprika)
- 1½ tablespoons salt (feel free to add more if you like your seasoning salty)
- 2 teaspoons red pepper flakes
- 2 teaspoons oregano (we like Mexican oregano)

38. **Halloween Costumes.** These are the quintessential single-use clothing items that are perfect to share once you're done with them. They're also the original and one of the best DIY parent-child bonding projects ever. So, get your crafty juju on and start figuring out how to make that Godzilla costume. Or wait until a few weeks before Halloween and ask for what you're looking for. You'll probably find it in someone else's closet, and they'll gratefully off-load it on your doorstep.

39. **Planters and Trellises.** If it holds stuff, it can be a planter. You just have to use your imagination and choose food-safe containers for edible plants. We've seen bras, toilets, bike helmets, hollowed-out tree stumps, bathtubs, toy trucks, paint cans, and baby shoes double as planters. Just get creative! Like planters, trellises are a garden feature that can include whimsical Reuse. We've been known to use sticks, iron bed headboards, bicycle wheels, upside-down patio umbrellas (without the fabric), metal benches, macramé tablecloths, chain-link fencing, lamp stands, old chairs, picket fencing, and of course chicken wire. If you don't have any of these things or are aiming for a specific look, you can source planters secondhand through your gift economy.

40. **Seedling Starter Pots.** Skip the plastic starter pots and use cardboard egg cartons or toilet paper tubes cut in half as mini plant pots for seedlings.

MICROPLASTICS, MACRO PROBLEM

Recent attention to the problem of plastic in the oceans has focused on the North Pacific Gyre, the "garbage patch" of plastics believed to be twice the size of Texas. Yet now the problem of human-generated plastics in the ocean has been tracked to all five of our globe's gyres, the massive circular current systems in the North and South Pacific Oceans, the North and South Atlantic, and the Indian Ocean. Plastic photodegrades over centuries, breaking up into minuscule bits that eerily mimic the look of zooplankton, those microorganisms that play a critical role in aquatic food webs. We know that microplastics in the marine environment now outnumber zooplankton, and they're working their way up the food web into our own bodies.

Dr. Joel Baker, the science director at the Center for Urban Waters in Tacoma, uses special nets, called manta trawls, behind boats in Puget Sound to catch a sampling of all things floating in the water. Researchers have found that more than 65 percent of the plastic on beaches is actually microscopic plastic debris.[18] So this means that if you took a random surface sampling of plastics on the beach, sifting through the sand and collecting every bit of it that was plastic, for every one hundred pieces, sixty-five of them would be too small for us to see without a microscope. But for filter feeders, like mussels, it looks like food. Scientists are currently amassing data to document how microplastics may be more biologically available to organisms that feed on plankton than plankton itself. This could be a problem if we eat those organisms. A recent study of fish in the North Atlantic revealed they ingest as much as twenty-four thousand tons of plastic debris each year.[19] The writing is on the wall: if fish and mussels are eating plastics, so are we.

41. **Fire Starters.** These are so easy to make, and they're a fun gift for kids to make. Save your dryer lint and cardboard egg cartons and then go to page 156 for our instructions.

42. **Puzzles.** When you've pored over a one-thousand-piece puzzle for a few days, do you really think you'll do it again? Probably not immediately. So get one from your neighbor! We have a strong ethic here in the Pacific Northwest where people share their two-thousand-, one-thousand-, and five-hundred-piece puzzles from home to home come wintertime.

43. **Furniture/Floor Protectors.** So many items can be used to protect your floors from the scratching legs of your furniture. Thinly sliced wine corks, old flip-flops, or shoe sole inserts are perfect for this. Just cut them to size and add a little glue.

44. **Tampons.** Use a menstrual cup. It's a onetime purchase, and it should save you multiple trips to the store to buy more tampons. Worth every penny you'll spend.

45. **Long Matches.** If you already have a flame source, like a pilot light, and you just need long matches to light certain candles or an oven pilot light, use a long dry piece of spaghetti or fettuccine pasta! It works perfectly.

46. **Air Freshener.** Take a cue from Rebecca's Grandma Inge, and use a cup or bag of freshly used coffee grounds as a room deodorizer or car air freshener (toss them into your garden as compost after a day or two). Tea leaves, orange peels, and bowls of fresh or dry lavender work well, too, as does a glass or bowl of white vinegar. A small jar filled with baking soda and a dozen drops of your favorite essential oil is another good recipe.

47. **Baby Wipes.** When our babies were babies, we used a spray bottle with water and clean "wiping towels," which were essentially soft rags, to wipe our babies' booties. We ran it by our pediatricians and they gave the seal of approval for this practice, especially since the littles hopped into the tub every few nights. Some parents like to add a tiny bit of a neutral oil (one that can't go rancid), a little liquid baby soap or shampoo, and a couple of drops of essential oil to the bottle.

48. **Firewood.** Where we live, there are winter windstorms. Big trees and branches come down all the time. If you're willing to haul it away, most people are happy to have you take the wood off their property. Our friend Ingrid's father is famous for popping on his bright knit cap and hitting the roads after storms, picking up fallen branches from the public right-of-way. He heats his home and helps clear storm debris from the roads, all for free.

49. **Balloons.** Balloons blow. They really do. Set them free, along with the ribbon they're attached to, and they'll end up in a tree or out in the ocean, the ribbon wrapping itself around some seaweed, possibly entangling a seal or sea turtle. Rather than using balloons for your festive events, try

colorful bunting instead. Bunting can be Reused and made of fabric scraps so they won't blow away with the wind and become litter or a hazard. We make ours from fabric remnants and bias tape, no sewing required if you use a bead of fabric glue down the center of the tape.

DIY FABRIC BUNTING

- Collect some fabric. For visual excitement, pick a pleasing assortment of colors and patterns. Some possibilities include old sheets, stained tablecloths, scraps from a quilter or seamstress friend, and favorite clothing that's ready for the ragbag but that deserves better.
- Find some extra-wide double-fold bias tape, one three-yard piece per banner. You can find directions to make your own online.
- You'll need some craft or fabric glue if you want to make this as a no-sew project.
- Make a pattern. A basic semicircle works with the flat side running nine inches wide by six and a half inches tall. This size works well with three yards of bias tape, leaving enough tape on the ends to attach string for hanging, or to pin into. Some people prefer classic triangle pennant shapes, or rectangles hung by their short side, or a mixture of shapes. Pick your own favorite.
- Iron your fabrics, then trace your pattern piece onto your fabric. Use pinking shears to cut out the bunting flags.
- Decide how you want to arrange your fabrics, then open up that bias tape and start to glue the fabric into place,

one piece at a time. Set the straight edge of your fabric pieces even with the inside crease of the bias tape. Before you place the fabric onto the bias tape, put a thin bead of glue on the bottom of the tape, then add another thin bead on top of the fabric and fold the top of the bias tape down flat onto the fabric. Run your fingers over the freshly glued area, pressing gently to stick everything together, then move along to the next piece. It's a good idea to lay everything out before you start the gluing so that you can center the fabric well and leave some bias tape free on either side. As you glue, snug the fabric pieces up so their edges just touch, and set the whole thing where it can dry flat.

- You have fabric bunting that can be tied or pinned into place, indoors or out, good for years of festive decorating. If you'd like machine-washable bunting, skip the glue and stitch everything into place instead. But we've been able to decorate years of parties now without having to wash our glued-together bunting, and nothing has fallen apart when left out in the rain and damp overnight.

50. **Garlic Press.** Skip the kitchen gizmo and use a pestle-shaped stone instead. Liesl's used one in her kitchen for fifteen years now. In Nepal, her friends use two stones in their kitchens, a flat one that acts as a board and a cylindrical one for crushing, mashing, and grinding garlic, chili peppers, whole grains, or whole spices on top of the flat stone. Next time you see a pestle-shaped stone out in the woods, in your garden, or on the bank of the nearest river or stream, consider using it as your garlic press. Think caveman, not Crate & Barrel. One hit on the garlic and it's peeled. Another smash and it's crushed. Easy.

Make Every Day a Special Occasion

Do you have treasures stashed away for "special occasions"? How often do you use them? We thought so. It's time to take these lovely things out of storage. Life is too short, and yes, you're worth it!

As the parents of baby boomers pass away, their belongings are being redistributed among families, and many of us may find ourselves gifted with an old set of good china that we feel duty bound to store away. We're so scared of losing or damaging our nice things that we're missing out on the true joy of them. Why? Liesl's been using her great-grandmother's best china for years, even with school-age kids, and even for the simplest meals. They can be put in the dishwasher, so there's really no reason not to use them. And, yes, one was broken a year or so ago and it was glued back together. Looks pretty much as good as new and has some character now.

Natalya Peskin from Redmond, Washington, writes about how sad it can be to not use our inherited items: "Several times I had

121

a duty of going through things of deceased family members. The hardest things to see were these 'special items' they were stashing somewhere. One of the saddest ones were wineglasses that my MIL displayed and never used. They came from her MIL, who also displayed and never used them. There were also nice German and English dishes. When we came over, my in-laws usually served food in old plastic dishes from a garage sale."

Seek out special items gathering dust in your cabinets and closets and start enjoying them today!

- **Clothing.** Stop saving your nice clothing for special occasions. If something makes you feel great, just wear it—for a meeting, for work, for dinner with friends. If you start wearing the good stuff, you won't need so much of the not-so-good stuff.
- **Jewelry.** Put on that bracelet you haven't worn for years or those earrings you hide away to avoid losing. They can't bring you joy if you don't wear them. If you realize you'll never wear many of the things you've been storing away, seize the moment and give it to someone you love. Now is better than never. They'll always think of you when they wear it.
- **Makeup/Perfume/Toiletries.** Make today a spa day. Liesl had some peppermint foot oil that she's been saving—for a day when she could put her feet up—since she gave birth to her son sixteen years ago. There it sat, in her bathroom cabinet. It has moved with her family three times, and all the way across the country. Finally, she realized it was time to use that stuff up! Use your bath oil, bubble bath, your exfoliating cream, your incense, your best perfume. These things just don't get better with age.

- **Food.** Now's the time to get into your pantry and pull out the stuff that's been waiting for some special occasion. Use it up as best you can now, before it expires and has to be fed to someone's chickens.

- **Vases.** Don't let these sit unused in a cabinet! Use vases to display your collection of beach glass or river rocks, the contents of your family's pockets on laundry days (an interesting visual time capsule), feathers, twigs, marbles, all of the pocket change you save from Buying Nothing . . . and, of course, flowers.

- **Candles.** Candles can elevate a weeknight dinner into something special. Don't save those long-stem candles for an occasion that might not present itself. Use them now, and ask for more (or make your own) when they burn out.

- **Wineglasses.** Get out the crystal! Don't save these for the fancy dinners you might host someday. Drink your fine wine, kombucha, or sparkling water in nice glasses because it makes you feel fancy and sophisticated. Rebecca's kids grew up drinking water from fancy Buy Nothinged glasses and only broke one—special glasses inspire careful handling and last longer than you might expect.

- **Silverware.** If you're lucky enough to have it, use it! Don't let it sit and tarnish in storage. Eat a meal a week with it. Or, go rad and use it for all of your meals! How silly it is to have something special boxed up and not enjoyed.

- **Journals.** Have you bought several beautiful, inspiring journals only to store them for years on a bookshelf because you don't yet have that perfect thing to write? Just write! You can also use this for daily lists, work to-dos, and note taking.

- **Linens.** Do you even store away your best comforter, bedspread, pillows, sheets, linen napkins, for that rare occasion your aunt Eustace might come visiting? Use the best ones you can find for yourself! Don't save them for that special person or special time, because that person is you and the time is *now*!

Only the best for you. Starting right now.

We Invite You to Reuse & Refuse

We have three Reuse and Refuse challenges for you.

First up, Refuse: Choose five things from the 50 Things We Never Buy list, things that you can Refuse to buy without hardship or hassle. This should not be daunting—Refusing to buy should simplify your life and improve your mood and budget, not bring you suffering. Start with the items that meet this standard. Once you've got the first five items worked out of your regular shopping, add another batch. Add your own ideas to the list and share them in the buynothinggeteverything.com discussion forum.

Next up, Reuse: For one day, keep ahold of the SUDs (single-use disposables), product packaging, and paper items you would usually throw into a trash or recycling bin. Don't worry, you won't have to keep it forever, we want you to look for three items you can Reuse. Common everyday candidates include jars and bottles both glass and plastic; bags both paper and plastic; to-go chopsticks, forks, and spoons; greeting cards; junk mail; and nonconfidential work papers. Even when we're actively working to Refuse SUDs, they tend to find their way into our lives. Turn the tables on the system and Reuse these things. Jot your shopping list or journal entry on the back of junk mail or that meeting agenda; use those chopsticks from lunch to stake up your droopy houseplant; use that bag of shredded paper to cushion that box of snacks you're mailing to your niece in college. You can even turn this into an impromptu Give: fill that empty kombucha bottle with fresh water, pop in a pretty single flower, and leave it on a coworker's desk just for the joy of giving away a bit of free beauty.

Finally, spread the word. In order to harness the transformational power Refusing and Reusing can have on us and our planet, we need to celebrate your clever new workarounds and MacGyvering. You can make this happen by sharing a photo of your favorite Refuse or Reuse achievement, and ask others to share theirs. Do this in our buynothinggeteverything.com forum or in person, write about it in the margins of this book, which you can share with others, or add it to the agenda of any meeting you oversee as an icebreaker; work it into your life wherever it best fits for you. We promise, people find Refusing and Reusing fascinating once they've been given permission to talk about it.

STEP 4: REFLECT

When we use the words *Buy Nothing*, we aren't suggesting you deprive yourself of the things you need or love. In this step, we're asking you to pause and Reflect before you buy. This step is key to cultivating a Buy Nothing mind-set that will come to life through your actions. Before you buy something, ask yourself a simple question: Is there another way I can meet this need or desire, or must I buy this? There are times when, yes, you will need to buy things, but there are so many other options!

This is where non-buyerarchical thinking is your friend. All Buy Nothing options have equal value, each useful in its own time and place. Here are just a few: Do without. Find an alternative you already own. Make it. Borrow it. Ask for a used one. Ask for a brand-new one. Rent it. Buy it secondhand. Buy a reusable or durable, multiuse version. Picking an option will quickly become second nature, and your answers will vary based on all sorts of circumstances and variables. This is all good!

Every time we make a choice that puts an item that's already circulating among people to use, that's one less brand-new item being produced and distributed, using finite resources and adding to pollution along the way. And there are more of these options available every year; in addition to thousands of local gift economy groups full of new and used free things, there are rental options for everything from clothing to furniture and many international secondhand online markets. When you decide that you do truly need to buy a brand-new whatever it is, you'll be making a well-thought-out purchase that is highly unlikely to leave you with buyer's remorse. We think of Buy Nothing as a verb, a call to action, a lifestyle that shows you, if you look closely enough and put a little effort into it, that you'll actually find just what you were looking to buy in the first place. There truly is abundance all around us.

You'd be surprised at how much you can get without stepping foot in a store. It's a bad news–good news sort of thing: we've reached this point where there are so many durable goods in our environment, not just corralled in landfills or recycling centers (bad), that you can find almost everything you need, if you only ask or look (good). In addition to the sharing networks we've been discussing for many things, a variety of basic pocket and handbag items—such as pens, hair ties, rubber bands, pencils, and paperclips—are everywhere, in parking lots, outside schools, on roads and sidewalks. Our Earth now supplies not just food and shelter, but modern office supplies and more. And our kids will be the first to tell you that shopping this way is a lot more fun than any trip to the store—it's a free treasure hunt, complete with the rush of adrenaline that comes with the thrill of discovery. We get that some parents just won't be down with their kids picking up office supplies from parking lots. This isn't the only way to Buy Nothing.

Both of us often go for at least a year without buying a single garment, because our giving networks supply us with more clothes than we could ever need through round-robins and "clothing shares." Round-robins are sharing networks that get started when one person cleans out their closet, puts their discards (clothes they've outgrown or never wear) in a box, and passes it along to the next person on the list. The box travels down the list, going home with each host in turn, who takes what they'd like and adds whatever their own closet is ready to shed. Round-robins are great for kitchen items, gardening tools, stuffed animals, toddler toys, and even toiletries, but they're most effective for sharing clothing.

For those who work in corporate or professional environments, round-robins can be hugely helpful in varying their wardrobe without overspending on low-quality clothes. In many instances, their jobs depend on it. We recognize that for upwardly mobile women, buying a first suit or a special outfit is a powerful rite of passage. When you find these important wardrobe additions through clothes swaps, you get things that fit and flatter you, empowering you to rise at work while also freeing up your hard-earned wages. Swapped clothing also comes with the added value of well wishes and networking opportunities with the women you meet.

So it's not that we don't *get* new things. We just don't *buy* them. We find our stuff through gifting networks. We believe you can feel the same amount of euphoria acquiring something for free that's used as you would if you were buying it new. There's an argument that you can feel even more joy for having scored such a bargain. (Bargain and discount shoppers, take note!) We also realize that for true shopaholics out there, this may sound like a unique form of torture. Before you panic, read on.

The Thrill of Shopping

We know that some people just love the whole shopping experience in general. Perhaps you're one of them. You may buy at least one article of clothing a week, either going out to the stores to find that perfect bargain or sitting at home and shopping easily for wardrobe perks online. In an article in the *Atlantic* about how we are all accumulating mountains of things, the American Apparel and Footwear Association is credited with determining that in

2017, Americans spent, on average per person, $971.87 on clothes, buying nearly sixty-six garments, about 20 percent more than they spent in 2000.[1] The average Briton, likewise, according to the *Great British Wardrobe Report*, spends about £1,042 on new clothes and shoes each year.[2]

For many of us, there is an undeniable thrill to shopping, to acquiring new things. It feels good to buy things we want and need. There are many joys in shopping: the sense of sleuthing out hidden treasures for ourselves; the power and security of providing for our families; the excitement of finding that perfect gift for a loved one; the pride that comes from buying the things we need to succeed in our jobs, like the right clothes and symbols of power and competence. That good feeling you get when you find that perfect summer dress isn't just in your head; each of these purchases we make sets off that dopamine hit in our bodies each time we anticipate the reward of owning something new. Our online habits make it that much easier to shop and also make us more vulnerable to targeted advertising—those ads that follow you around on social media and on Google are designed with you in mind. We believe we've seen this same dopamine cycle in action in every single person participating in a gift economy. It's not the buying that matters, it's the anticipation of the reward, of the treasure, that has impact. When we receive that reward as a freely given gift from a friend or neighbor, it comes with benefits shopping can't compete with.

The other thing to keep in mind is the flip side of that dopamine hit: the feeling of letdown that comes soon after we bring our shiny new things home. Often that must-have purchase—that shoe, vase, or table we just knew was going to make our homes perfect, that thing we needed to be happy, or to feel secure, special, powerful, or loved—loses its shine after we own it. After sitting in your home for a bit, that candle holder or accent mirror quickly loses that special newness as you realize it does not have the magical powers you'd hoped it would. It hasn't transformed your life or your living space; it is just one more thing taking up space in your closet or home.

This is where gift economies are at their most powerful: when we've held a clothing swap with friends to rebuild our wardrobes, when we've received new kitchen tools or home decor or books from a neighbor, we have both the new-to-us things *and* we have new human connections. Even if we give and receive gifts without meeting up in person, through such things as quick front porch or office desk pickups, the fact that we've reached out to one another and met one another's needs has a depth that buying can seldom, if ever, match. Each transaction builds a new strand in a network of interconnection making us more secure, more seen, heard, and valued within the real world. We believe *this* is the magic many of us are looking for. We fill our shopping carts to fill a void that comes from disconnection. We're essentially shopping for the wrong thing in the wrong place. We can still be maximalists—there's no need to go without things you want or need—but you'll address a deeper need by Buying Nothing than you will through ordinary purchasing.

But what about those of us who just really, truly love to shop, or love to "want" something and then find an excuse to shop for it? Perhaps for you, it's all about the thrill of the hunt. You love the challenge of searching, finding, conquering, and gathering whatever it is your family "needs" at the time. Or maybe you love the thrill of finding a deal on that thing you want, purchasing it for the least amount of money. We know through many studies that dopamine is triggered in anticipation of buying something new, but we also have witnessed the sheer joy people feel when they are given the very things they are seeking, for free and from real people nearby. So let's take a moment to pause and look deeply at our "wants," the things we long to purchase, and the reasons beneath that desire. What you find may surprise you.

Step 4: Reflect

By now, we hope you've embraced Give, Ask, Reuse, and Refuse. It's time to Reflect. We each have complicated relationships with our stuff, and each Buy Nothing step has a way of illuminating this complexity. Reflecting can be one of the most surprising and revealing steps on your Buy Nothing journey.

Some of us don't have the financial luxury to prioritize our wants over our needs; the little cash buying power we have is focused on the true necessities of life. For these readers, Buying Nothing can bring security and safety and a renewed sense of respect when we receive things we need, things we want but could never buy, and when we have a chance to give to others on equal footing.

Some of us are so overwhelmed by demands on our time and energy that we purchase things whenever possible because it seems like the easiest way to meet our kid-spouse-family-home-work-friends responsibilities. If you purchase those goggles for swim lessons on the train to work, you've crossed one thing off your endless to-do list before the day has even begun. For these convenience shoppers, Buying Nothing can bring a shift in actions in which our stuff does double or triple duty for us through Reuse and sharing so that we have fewer items to purchase, dispense, dispose of, purchase again, and so on. Asking for goggles in your gift economy only takes a few seconds.

Some of us are buying things to fill voids in our lives, to remind ourselves that we are beautiful, smart, worthy of friendship and attention, of use to others, and good enough in our own right to deserve lives of meaning and joy. For us, Buying Nothing can turn interactions around old stuff into new friendships, new social and support networks, entertainment, and a chance to exercise our innate generosity to build a community we enjoy living in.

Whatever stories your stuff holds, whatever your stuff represents to you, Buying Nothing promises you plenty of opportunities to learn about yourself and to increase your happiness, both with your stuff and with yourself. We know this might sound like a double standard, but please bear with us: we want you to ask for everything your heart desires, and we want you to examine what's at the core of your desire for stuff, more stuff. We each have conscious needs and wants, and we each have hidden, subconscious needs that drive many of our "wants." When we expose these hidden parts of ourselves, we can take control of our accumulation and let go of stuff.

Maybe partaking in a gift economy strikes you as chaotic or time-consuming, so you opt to buy things instead. Efficiency in obtaining what we need is important to every busy working person's life, and at first glance, a human-connection-centered gift economy may seem to be much less time efficient than a profit-centered market economy is. As you establish a giving network around yourself, it may indeed take longer to source a needed item through your network than to purchase it in an instant online. We can't argue with you there. But we've seen with our own eyes, too many times to count, how swiftly gift economies can meet needs and wants once they're active and established. We frequently see gifts requested, received, and picked up all in the same hour or afternoon or evening, beating even next-day shipping or a trek to the nearest shopping center. Setting up this sort of network does take an initial investment of time, giving, and asking on your part. We encourage you to take some time now to identify Buy Nothing actions you find easy and pleasant so that you can start to build strong everyday giving connections, at your own rate.

We're all familiar with the old adage "You get what you pay for," and we have a Buy Nothing version of it: "You get the community you invest in." Buying Nothing gives us each a chance to put our resources where our values are. If you're in it for free stuff, you'll definitely get that. If you're looking to declutter, you'll find takers for your things (and grateful new friends along the way). If you'd like to spend less time driving to shopping malls or searching e-commerce sites, you'll achieve these objectives. And meeting all of these goals comes with an added value: Buying Nothing helps build a more connected, compassionate world that you will enjoy living in. You won't even need to invest your money, just your old stuff, your skills, and your time asking for things before shopping. These investments will reap all sorts of dividends and rewards. It may feel inefficient at first as you build sharing network habits that are very different from shopping. Once these new habits become second nature, and buying things becomes the last resort instead of the first automatic action, you will discover the various efficiencies at work in a human-centered gift economy. Here's one example from millions of Buy Nothing actions, broken down to help you think about how to identify your own investments and rewards so that you can target your Buy Nothing resources and energy where they'll do the most work for you:

It's your child's birthday and she's big on pirates, so you want to throw a pirate-themed party. You put it out to your giving group that you're looking for pirate booty (not the popcorn kind) for an eight-year-old's party. A neighbor just finished with a similar-themed party and drops the paper swords, bandanas, and hats off on your doorstep, happy to off-load them. Others have pirate flags, costumes, and fun read-aloud books. Someone even offers to bake a pirate cake in their ship-shaped cake pan. Done! While you had to go through the effort to ask and coordinate getting all of the stuff, you saved a trip to a few different stores, and the time you would have spent researching products online. Plus everyone else enjoyed participating in their own small ways. And your child, of course, was thrilled to have the party of her dreams; she felt loved, much more from your stress-free presence than from the pirate plunder.

Remember the UCLA study of thirty-two middle-American family homes and the objects they counted? There were a stupendous number of items in each home, some three hundred thousand of them, so many that the mothers were feeling stressed from all that clutter. So many that most had to store the excess in their new junk drawer, the garage. One of the interesting conclusions of the study was that the researchers found that only 25 percent of the household garages could actually be used to store cars since the spaces were jam-packed with household overflow. Many had shelves of bulk-bought items from big-box stores, enough bleach and toilet paper for half a year. Others had plans to sell stored keepsakes eventually, or to use them for projects that never materialized, like repairing them or renovating them. We'd posit that many households just go out and buy the very things they have stored in their garages and attics simply because it's too difficult to find anything or because they have forgotten they had it to begin with. (If this sounds like your garage, perhaps you can ask, in your giving group, for someone to help you manage your stuff.

We're sure you can find a person who is great at organizing and *loves* to do it.)

There's another benefit to asking versus buying. As you find the words to articulate your request, your brain will naturally engage in a bit of Reflection regarding whether you truly want or need that item. Frequently, the act of formulating an Ask inspires the discovery of a clever alternative you already have. And when you have decided that, yes, you do indeed want or need this new thing, it is often faster and easier to get it from a neighbor or friend, free of charge, than to spend the time online or in person to buy it. The time you invest in Asking and Reflecting, and in picking up gifts instead of buying things, will pay off in obvious ways (free stuff! new friends!) and in deeper, less tangible ways that will reveal themselves more fully over time.

When we take the time to Reflect before we buy and to Ask instead of purchase, we become more connected with the stories and emotions that are hidden in our stuff. We will understand ourselves better and be ready to make informed and joyful decisions about our possessions, bringing ourselves peace of mind when we let go of things, ask for what we want and need, and share more.

LIESL'S TABOO DRESS

I was the youngest in a four-kid family, and everything that was mine once belonged to my siblings. I rarely had a thing of my own that hadn't already been played with or worn. What was mine was really theirs by default, and the things that were theirs—in true sibling style—I was often forbidden to touch.

As a teenager, I coveted my older sister's pink flapper-style polka-dot dress. I simply *loved* that dress, which she rarely wore. One summer day, when she was out of town, I sneaked into her closet and "borrowed" the dress to go out with friends. Despite feeling somehow perfect in that dress, imagining myself to be smart and beautiful like my big sister, I was so afraid of being caught that the pure joy of wearing it was taken away. I managed to put a minuscule stain on the dress that I thought could never be detected. A month later, from the tone of her voice as she came into my room with the dress clenched in her hands, I knew immediately what she had discovered. I don't think I had ever done anything so rotten to her. At the time, it seemed like she'd never forgive me.

That experience forever changed my relationship with stuff. I let go of my attachment to things. I didn't fully understand why, but it felt freeing. I gave and loaned things to others wholeheartedly and established strong bonds with friends who liked to trade and share what we had. I went so far as to loan out my most precious things, exploring the taut boundaries between holding on and letting go, and understood implicitly that the things I shared might never come back. My sister called this behavior irresponsible, and accused me of not taking care of my things. She was partly right. I was transfixed by the pleasure I experienced in sharing, letting go, and seeing what would happen in my relationships as a result.

Were they "my" things, or things to enjoy and connect me to others, even if I might lose the things in the end? As I was the youngest sibling, my things were never really mine to begin with, so I never felt the need to hold on to them. Giving away the few things that were mine—like a set of precious earrings I had purchased during a summer on Corsica or handmade dresses I'd sewn myself—was hard to do at first, until I let go of the thing itself and appreciated how happy my friend felt wearing them. There were so many earrings in the world. I could always make another dress. I learned that the more I gave away, the more I wanted to give away. The good feelings were addictive. I practiced taking all the power out of owning and coveting things. having seen the alienation and separation that can come with ownership. Coveting and hoarding tendencies made me anxious and propelled me to give all the more.

Thirty-odd years later, my experiment continues. The everyday things in my home are items given to us by neighbors passing along their excess. It feels natural to me, hand-me-downs that connect me to those closest to me, just as my siblings' things did. I wouldn't have it any other way, because now my own gifts are an expression of a lifetime of lessons learned about letting go and finding the pure satisfaction, serendipity, and joy that comes from sharing.

We Invite You to Reflect

When you practice Reflection, you gain access to your subconscious needs, desires, and anxieties, and can face them head-on. What's driving your daily, often mindless purchases? What's the hidden need behind the want? Is it loneliness, boredom, fear of scarcity, envy, fear of getting hurt emotionally, low self-esteem, or exhaustion?

Try working through this list of questions the next time you have something in hand to purchase:

Questions to Ask Before You Buy Something

1. How did you first see this item? Did you desire it and go searching for it or was it presented to you through marketing? Do you still need or want it now?

2. Do you plan to care for it for the rest of its useful life, including dry cleaning/dusting/washing/oiling/etc.? Do you still need or want it now?

3. Do you believe this item will make you healthier, stronger, more attractive, smarter? Are there nonconsumer choices to help you feel this way? Is it likely this item can deliver that result? Do you still need or want it now?

4. Where will you store this item, is there enough room for it, and will it be in the way of other items you need access to? Do you still need or want it now?

5. Can you make this item, or is there anything you already own that could substitute for it? Do you still need or want it now?

6. Are you willing to repair, or pay for repairing, this item when it breaks? Do you still need or want it now?

7. Are you replacing something you already have? What's wrong with the old one? Can the old one be fixed, cleaned, or upgraded? Do you still need or want it now?

8. Can you delay purchasing this item? For how long—a month, a year? Do you still need or want it now?

9. Do you really need this item now, or just want it? Is there a hidden need behind your want? If you have a hidden need, what is it, and can you find other nonconsumer ways to meet it? Do you still need or want it now?

10. So you've answered all of these questions so far and, yes, you do need this item. Is there an important reason you

need to spend money on it? If a free one would work, do you need to keep it forever, or could you ask to borrow one? Is there a safety reason it must be brand-new, never used? If so, could you ask for a brand-new one in your local gift economy? If a used one would work, could you ask for that? There are things that we do need, but even then, *need* and *need to buy* don't have to go together.

Pose these questions to yourself before purchasing the next thing you want to buy, and see if you can find the hidden need behind the want. It may help to journal your thoughts or talk through solutions with a friend or fellow gift group member. You might be surprised by how much you learn about yourself from this soul searching, and how much it helps to have a community to lean on as you make this a new Buy Nothing habit.

Here's another exercise to help you identify hidden needs that compel your shopping (it's especially powerful when done with a friend or two). Imagine that you could have anything, anything at all, that you wanted and everything you need. Make a list, think *big*, and include tangible and intangible things. Then set your list aside, take a break, and come back to see what your ultimate wish list says about the stuff and the life you want. Are any of the tangible things on your list connected to happy memories from your life, are they your own private symbols of bigger, less tangible needs? Are there things or skills you could ask for to help you attain the intangible things on your list? Are you looking for more time to yourself, more time with family or friends, more adventure, more security, less stress? Keep what you learn about yourself in mind as you're looking for stuff to bring home and stuff to give away.

STEP 5: MAKE & FIX

The word *economics* comes from the ancient Greek word first used by Aristotle, *oikonomos*, meaning "household management." In most premodern societies, production and consumption occurred in the household, and running such an economy meant stewarding resources to ensure that everyone's needs were met. This immediately translated into the greater good of the community, where the goal was not to generate winners and losers, but the healthy functioning of the whole so that the community could preserve their way of life, the good life.

We embarked on this way of life because we felt so helpless in the midst of all the marketing coming our way, in every form: in our homes, through the internet, and out in our towns and cities every time we walk into a supermarket or store. Advertising promotes a culture of competition, with winners and losers, at the expense of the whole. Ads tend to manipulate your fears and make you imagine a world filled with scarcity instead of abundance: "Come and get it while supplies last." And when we saw the result of all of this consumption—the waste washing up on our beautiful beaches—we got angry. And we turned that anger and angst into the power to control what we purchased and brought into our own homes. We were not helpless.

In many countries, including the US, a small number of people control the vast majority of the wealth, which means the rest of us earn what's left. For example, in the US, the top 1 percent holds more wealth than the middle class.[1] Mass-produced plastic goods tend to be manufactured for the middle and lower classes, cheap goods made on a colossal scale to be consumed by those who can afford only the cheapest products, products that are not made to last. Many of us buy cheap manufactured goods to meet our budgets, things that last for only a few uses, because we are afraid we wouldn't be able to survive without them. We're told they make everyday life easier for us. But the more we use them, the more we trash our environment, filling our landfills with them, polluting our waters and burning more fossil fuels to make them, and warming the climate. These goods don't necessarily make our lives easier. We have to buy them, manage them, and then figure out what to do with them when they inevitably break.

Imagine what kind of impact we could have on our expenses and the environment if we not only shared more but made more of our own things instead of buying them?

Be a Producer, Not a Consumer

Millennials have brought back an old way of living with a hip new name: maker culture. Maker culture is one that prizes the ability to fix old and worn items and patch together new creations from existing supplies. This lost art would be very familiar to many of our ancestors, not all that many generations back. And this attitude is key to a Buy Nothing lifestyle—and infuses the challenge with an irresistible dose of creativity.

It's hard to put a price on the work you do, if you love doing it. If you're like most people, you're not paid to do what you truly love. In a recent survey put together by the founder of LinkedIn, 46 percent of baby boomers, 16–31 percent of Gen Xers, and only 12 percent of millennials had their "dream job."[2] Buying Nothing is the perfect reason to unleash your inner baker, knitter, crafter, painter, engineer, electrician, and car mechanic. We've seen many people of all ages share their hidden talents in their local giving networks. Because there's no compensation involved, there is a freeing lack of pressure, which seems to support creativity and innovation.

Our friend Myra Zocher has a talent for baking. Her handmade sourdough seed bread is delicious. In the early days of our first local gift economy, Myra regularly baked bread for the community and gave away the big boules, with seeds, like an everything bagel, pressed and baked lightly into their crusts. Liesl filmed her baking process one day and went home with a sense of awe over the love and hands-on care that goes into each loaf. Thanks to the overwhelmingly positive feedback she received from us all, Myra now has a successful local bakery, A Woman Sconed. Don't be afraid to share your gifts and chase your dreams, because if you don't share your art, your talents, or your handmade products, you won't feel the gratitude the world can show you for being who you are. You may never know what your gifts are if you don't share them.

Ask yourself, what are you good at? Do you sew, or knit, are you great at giving massages, do you quilt or bake, garden, or just have a great listener's ear? Make what you love. Stop consuming the things that are better made than bought. Just say no to being a consumer of mass-produced items. And, better yet, make so many of your best products that you have enough to give so that other people can enjoy them without buying, too.

Step 5: Make

What do you love to do or create? What have you been buying that you could make instead? Now is the time to think about what makes you passionate—what sort of activity you could do for the pure pleasure of doing that might result in something nice to keep in your home or give to friends. We all feel busy and overtasked, but if you take the time to create for the sake of creating, the benefits will come back to you in ways you can't yet imagine. If you can't think of something to "produce," explore new-to-you things you can make, with things you have in excess or that are readily available. Experiment!

If you love to cook or bake, start by making large batches of your best meals, or desserts. Freeze them or give them away. A homemade meal is a thoughtful gift when someone moves into a new home or has a new baby, or just because! Some of us are more artistically inclined, so creating beautiful mosaic stepping-stones from broken ceramics, or painted rocks for a garden, or colorful rag rugs for a bathroom floor could be your thing. There's so much we can do and share from the excess around us. Find the things that come easily to you, and create from them.

Liesl's daughter Cleo has a green thumb. Her thriving succulent plants spill from the garden into the driveway and plant themselves there. Inspired by the appealing planters she noticed at the local nursery—sedums whimsically arranged in ceramics, wooden boxes, shoes, even children's boots—Cleo has started creating her own arrangements. When she has a little time, she collects the sedums and plants them into all sorts of found objects around the house, like teacups, and then gives them away. The gifts are a living testimony to what we can creatively do with the excess around us. A friend of ours always makes extra spaghetti sauce and gives it away. Yet another asks friends to save up their liquid laundry soap dispensers so that when she runs out, she makes an extra batch or two of her special laundry soap recipe and gives them as gifts. Everyone loves something homemade!

Don't feel like you need to go spend a bunch of money at a craft store—remember, we're all about Buying Nothing. Part of the fun is locally sourcing the materials, ideally from items found or given for free. You'd be surprised at how abundantly available these raw materials can be when you think creatively. Not only does this re-purpose material that would otherwise wind up in landfills, but it keeps your costs low. If you have plum trees in your yard or a local park that no one picks from, you can make plum preserves to give away. You might have a carpenter friend who is always try-ing to get rid of wood scraps. These remnants can be the basis of something you like making, like birdhouses, small planter boxes, or a big bonfire of untreated wood for friends in a firepit you made from the metal basket inside an old washing machine. Take a look at what you're throwing away and that might be the very thing someone else truly wants! Yes, your waste may be another's want.

Buying Nothing doesn't mean living a life of minimalism or austerity (unless that floats your boat). We can be maximalists and enjoy extravagance while also respecting the Reduce and Re-fuse Rs when we harness our ability to make for ourselves and to share. Truly, there is *so much stuff* already in existence awaiting creative Reuse and sharing.

Fix It!

There's yet another R that's an important part of the Buy Noth-ing lexicon: Repair. If there were no stores near you, if you lived far from commerce, you'd fix whatever you could. Our throwaway culture tends to just toss things in favor of buying new, mostly because we've lost the skills necessary to fix our broken stuff. But thanks to Google and YouTube, you can learn how to fix just about everything. When the repair is beyond your skills or tools (even with assistance from the internet), reach out to your giving network to ask for help. We've seen neighbors rescue one another from plumbing, appliance, auto, fashion, and carpentry disasters of all sorts.

There's also beauty in some broken things. In Japan, there's an art form called *kintsugi*, where broken ceramics are repaired with a lacquer mixed with gold, silver, and other precious metals, bringing attention to the very breaks that occurred. Use this as inspiration the next time you break something decorative—perhaps you can make it into something beautiful.

The more we mend, the less we spend. Sign up for courses or ask a friend to teach you how to fix electronics, cars, or clothing. Look around for events where people fix things. Portland, Oregon, hosts three Fix-It Fairs each year. You can bring an item in to be fixed, and experts are there to try to help salvage whatever it is that needs servicing. Prince Edward Island has a Fix It Fair. In the UK, the Restart Project teaches skills for repairing electronics, and there is a physical place called the Edinburgh Remakery, where you can bring your items in to be fixed and learn the skills to do it yourself. There may also be neighbors around you who are good at fixing things, who wouldn't mind if you asked. Go ahead and ask for help and see if someone steps up.

Michelle Lee, a mom who lives in Ellicott City, Maryland, was full of gratitude when her neighbor's husband volunteered to help fix the slide attached to the swing set in her backyard. For weeks, the kids hadn't been able to use it, but with a few tools and a spare piece of lumber, he was able to get it back into service.

Celebrate the age-old ethic of fixing what we already have by learning how to darn a sock, repair a sewing machine, replace the parts of a leaky toilet, revive a dead vacuum cleaner, or wire a broken old lamp. Sew a button, patch a bike tire. Mend your blown-out flip-flops or replace a broken shovel handle. You'll feel empowered, having averted the need to buy new, by repairing the perfectly fixable things in our midst. That old thing can likely still keep working if we just gain some skills, do a little research, and believe in our ability to fix our things and steward them into long life. Then, share your fix-it stories with everyone so they'll be inspired, too, to fix the next thing that breaks in their home.

50 Things We Make

If you need more inspiration, here's a list of some of the gifts or products we like to make. These things cost us almost nothing, but they're useful things we may use every day, and they make great gifts for friends and family. This is just a list to get you started—there are hundreds of things you can make, and often your homemade staples like ketchup, yogurt, and mayonnaise are better than anything you can get in the store. Don't take this list as a mandate, either. Start small. Choose two or three things to make, and see if they help you to buy less, waste less, and share more.

1. **Candles.** There's no need to buy beautiful candles when you can make them. Collect wax scraps from half-burned candles and turn them into large colorful candles to give

away as gifts or use at home when the power goes out. You can make candles in jars or cans, or borrow candle-making molds. Here's how:

- Gather up all of your collected candle wax from partly burned candles throughout the year and ask for used candles from your giving network. Using a hammer on a wooden board, crush the candle wax into pieces that will fit into your jar, can, or candle mold. Reserve some wax, ideally a contrasting color, to melt into the mold. Be sure to remove the wicks, setting them aside for your candle. (You can string multiple leftover wicks together, if needed.)
- Fill your glass jars, cans, or molds with your multicolored wax chunks, placing a wick in the center. Lay a pencil or pen across the mouth of the jar or mold and wrap the end of the wick around it, to keep it from falling in the wax.
- Take the reserved wax, melt it in a spare old saucepan that's just for crafting, and pour it into the jar or mold, being careful to keep the wick straight. The melting wax will mix with the wax chunks and blend into a pretty wax mosaic.
- Add a drop or two of your favorite essential oil for some aromatherapy.
- Let your jars, cans, or molds solidify and cool overnight. In the morning, your candle is ready! Trim the wick and pull the candle out of the mold if you used one. These make for great gifts.

2. **Perennial Splits.** Perennials are flowering plants that come

back after winter to bloom again each year. But, to keep them healthy and under control, splitting them in half can revive the old plant so it can put its energies into a smaller, more manageable plant. Japanese irises and daisies are always in need of splitting, so we share them with other gardeners each year.

3. **Fruit and Wine Vinegar.** We make pretty vinegars, use them throughout the year, and also give them away to friends and family. Fruit scrap vinegar, like blackberry vinegar or apple cider vinegar, is a DIY recipe that could change your buying habits. Vinegars are so easy to make, it's almost a crime to not make them with your leftovers. In a glass jar, combine two cups of leftover red wine with a cup of distilled water and some "mother" from a previous organic vinegar you've finished and cover the jar with cheesecloth or a clean piece of cotton cloth so air can get in and dust stays out. Keep the jar in a cool dark place, essentially at room temperature.

The "mother" is the live active culture that makes vinegar. If you look closely at the contents of an organic wine or fruit vinegar, you'll see a gelatinous mass in the bottom of the bottle. This is the live culture, a type of acetic-acid-producing bacteria called acetobacter that consumes the alcohol in your wine, converting it into delicious vinegar. You can use this culture as a starter for any vinegars you make. If you find yourself motherless, ask for one in your local gift economy (people will laugh along with you). Or you can find some in the bottom of any bottle of unfiltered raw organic apple cider vinegar. Save yours and use it over and over again. Apple cider vinegar is an essential ingredient in our homes. It'll cure you of any cold and is an excellent rinse for your hair. Save that mother, take care of it, and you'll be ready to start making your own vinegars.

To make fruit vinegars, save scrap apple peels and cores. Blackberries from our local roadside vines also make an incredibly delicious vinegar. Put the fruit scraps in a jar with some water and a mother from another vinegar, cover with cloth, and store at room temperature, out of the sun, allowing the vinegar to breathe.

Check on your jars periodically; it'll take a few weeks for the fermentation and culture to reach its peak. After about a month, run the vinegar and fruit mixture through a cheesecloth, separating out the fruit for composting. Be sure to save the mother and place it and the filtered vinegar into a pretty bottle and cork it! And as the vinegar ages, like all of us, it only gets better.

4. **Dryer Balls.** Collect old wool discards, like yarn and old sweaters, and turn them into dryer balls (as described on page 101). People love them! They're an alternative to dryer sheets and help reduce dryer time by at least 10 percent.

5. **Vegetable Stock.** See our recipe on page 113 for the easiest veggie stock to make, all from scraps you wouldn't have eaten anyway.

6. **Kombucha.** Make fruit-flavored kombuchas in pretty bottles and give them away. Easy instructions for making kombucha can be found on the internet. All you'll need is a huge mason jar, some tea, sugar, and the active culture called SCOBY (symbiotic culture of bacteria and yeast). They're very easy to find in your local gift economy, because they multiply!

7. **Refashioned Clothing.** If you're handy with a needle or sewing machine, you can of course make your own clothing from scratch. And even if you're not, like Rebecca, you can still refashion secondhand clothes into new wardrobe additions. She and her kids love doing this. There are a couple of tricks that help make this successful: Start with items that are too large, and be fearless. Use safety pins to experiment with hems, tucks, pleats, seams, and draping. When you like how a piece looks and fits, bring out the needle and thread. Do not be afraid to cut off things you don't like or to put multiple pieces together, to add or subtract as you desire. Rebecca's all-time favorite skirt is a combination of a 1960s lacy nightgown, a 1970s blouse, and some strips of a 1980s scarf. Be bold and see what happens. Tackling textile waste this way is a whole lot of fun and an excellent project to do with the kids.

8. **Pesto.** Any green herb is ready to be turned into pesto. Pick an herb, an oil, a nut, garlic (if desired), a bit of salt, Parmesan cheese, and lemon or lime juice. Blend it all together (a blender or food processor works well for this) and eat it fresh or freeze it for later. Some of our favorite combinations include watercress with almonds, dandelions and cress with macadamia nuts, parsley and cilantro with pine nuts and garlic, big-leaf maple blossoms with pistachios, and the classic basil (and even arugula as a substitute) with pine nuts or walnuts and garlic.

9. **Perfume.** If you have a favorite essential oil or blend of essential oils, turn it into a perfume. All you need is some vodka, just an ounce, and about twenty drops of your es-

sential oils. Put it in a tiny spray bottle, shake well, and, voilà, you have your own custom-made perfume!

10. **Eggs and Veggies.** Okay, our chickens and backyard gardens do this work, and we just take credit for it. We give away all of our excess produce and chicken eggs. Many cities and suburbs are rewriting codes to allow for a couple of hens per household, and there are more community gardens, allotments, and parking strip vegetable beds every year, empowering people to grow their own food. Even if there hasn't been a farmer in your family for generations, don't write this idea off. It's not hard, there are people eager to help you, there's evidence that touching or simply smelling soil may be a natural antidepressant,[3] and it's the best way ever to make new friends.

11. **Bread.** Every once in a while, Liesl's family bakes an extra loaf of bread, because they love their recipe so much, and either freeze it for later consumption or give it away. If you have a bread machine, just put these ingredients into it, in any order, using the machine's suggested timings, and you'll have a delicious bread to show for it: 1 cup warm water; ¾ cup combination of the following ingredients: 1 egg plus milk and a little yogurt; 2 tablespoons flaxseed oil (you can substitute a nut oil, but flaxseed oil is excellent); 1 heaping teaspoon salt (we use a Celtic sea salt); 3 cups flour (we prefer 1 cup whole wheat and 2 cups white, all organic); 4 handfuls of walnuts (or flaxseeds); 3–4 handfuls of raisins; 1 tablespoon honey; and ⅜ teaspoon yeast. And if you like a little body to your bread, add about ¼ cup shredded zucchini or carrots, which we do when those veggies are in the garden.

12. **Yogurt.** A couple of tablespoons of leftover yogurt make the perfect starter for a batch of homemade yogurt. Pour your favorite whole milk into a pot. There's no exact measurement for this, just pour as much milk as you want yogurt. (It's basically a one-to-one ratio of milk to finished yogurt.) Set your timer for about 8 minutes so the milk doesn't boil over. You want to heat up the milk until it scalds, meaning little bubbles start to appear on the sides of the pot, and a film develops on the surface. Turn off the heat and take the milk off the burner. Let it cool to room temperature. Add your 2 tablespoons yogurt and use a wire whisk to incorporate it completely into the milk. Pour the mixture into jars and place them into a pot of warm water to create a warm-water bath. You could put your pot of water over your pilot light on your stove, and that may be enough to keep the jars warm overnight. Or you could place the jars on a warm lintel above your fire in a towel or blanket for warmth (Rebecca goes low-tech and uses her plastic camping cooler, surrounding the jars of yogurt with jars of hot water, then closes the cooler lid tightly). The key is to find a spot that is consistently warm for 8–12 hours. The longer you let your yogurt mixture sit in the warmth, the firmer it gets. When it's the consistency you like, put it in the fridge to let it cool.

13. **Compost.** Compost is cooking in Liesl's backyard every day. Without these compost bins, she'd have a lot more trash, and would have to spend money on compost for her gardens that's easy to make right at home. If you have a big wooden box, it can suffice as a compost bin outside, and there are countertop units for those of us without yards; ask for one

in your gift economy. All of your kitchen scraps and organic waste can go into it, and a few weeks later you'll have beautiful compost. Learn more about what we put into our compost on page 237.

14. **Herbal Teas.** Lemon balm, mint, nettles, and chamomile grow out of control in our area. So we collect and dry them (in the sun or hung upside down indoors) and then save the dried herbs in pretty jars to use as teas throughout the year. Rebecca's daughter makes an amazing blend using laven-

der flowers, rose petals, and mint foraged from unsprayed neighborhood plants.

15. **Rag Rugs.** YouTube is your friend for this one. There are so many ways to make a rag rug, through braiding, finger crocheting, twisting, and knotting. Save up your favorite fabrics, clothing, bedding, even old pantyhose and socks! Rag rugs are an easy project that are a throwback to pioneer days when old worn-out clothes were repurposed in this way. We've seen beautiful rag rugs used as colorful accents for stepping out of the shower or bath and as comfy seat cushions at the kitchen table.

16. **Salad Dressings.** You're probably catching on here. Much of what we don't buy are simple things that we can make, so there will be some duplicates on these lists. Go to page 113 to get our recipe for an easy-peasy salad dressing to store in the fridge.

17. **Hair Detangler.** This is one of the easiest recipes that works for those hard-to-manage locks. If your child loves long hair but doesn't love to brush it, this stuff is for you. Put 1 tablespoon of your favorite oil or a combination of them, such as coconut—heated up, since it becomes solid at room temperature—avocado, apricot, olive, jojoba, and sweet almond, in ½ cup water in a pretty bottle that has a spray pump on the top of it. Add 1–2 drops of your favorite essential oil (try geranium, lavender, rosemary, rose, chamomile, peppermint, or grapefruit seed extract). For thicker hair, use more oil, as desired. Be sure to shake the bottle before spraying it. If your coconut oil solidifies, you can heat the detangler in your hand. This works especially well if you apply to wet hair before brushing.

18. **Fire Starters.** Put a jar by your dryer for collecting the lint you remove from it each cycle. When the jar is full of lint, stuff it into the cups of cardboard egg cartons with a single match standing up in the middle of each cup. We sometimes add bits of sawdust, pine needles, and shredded paper, too. If your family wears a mixture of synthetic and natural fibers like Rebecca's, your lint might not burn all that well, but other flammable household waste such as used matches, wood pencil shavings, and the odds and ends that collect in children's coat pockets (pretty leaves, sticks, and bits of torn tissues and paper) all work perfectly. Once your collection jar is full, melt wax in a craft pot and drip the melted wax over your lint mixture–stuffed egg cartons. Be sure to drip the wax next to the matches so that they stand upright. Let the wax harden. You've now made single-use fire starters that you can use by removing one cup at a time, embedding it in your fireplace with kindling and paper, and lighting the match to start your fire.

19. **Small Pet Bed.** Use a cardboard box and an old T-shirt to build a cozy hideaway for your cat or small dog. This works best with a large or extra-large men's-style T-shirt and a cardboard box around twelve to eighteen inches square. Fold in the flaps of the box or cut them off. Put the box inside the T-shirt so that the neckhole of the shirt sits centered over the opening of the box. Tie the bottom of the shirt together over the bottom of the box to keep the shirt on the box. Add another used T-shirt or other soft bedding to the inside of the box and set it down for your animal friend to discover. They'll be delighted to use the neckhole of the shirt as their door and window, and to have a box all to themselves. When

the box gets worn, break it down for recycling or garden use, wash the T-shirt, and make another.

20. **Chicken Bedding.** When you have chickens, you need chicken bedding. We've found that we can "make" our own with shredded paper! We ask for it in our community, and many are happy to give us their shreds. It composts perfectly, too, so long as there are no plastic bits in it. Cut grass works well, too.

21. **Slow-Cooked Beans.** Kick your canned beans habit and slow-cook dried pinto or black beans. It's so easy, you'll wonder why you hadn't done it before. You can make a large batch and then freeze your excess for future meals.

    To make your own beans, throw 4 cups rinsed beans into your slow cooker or a pot with a thick bottom with at least double the amount of water. Add 3–4 garlic cloves (you don't even have to peel them), some chopped onion, a large pinch of salt, and a bay leaf or two. Four cups of dried beans will result in about eight cups of cooked beans, enough for a family of four to enjoy for a week in many different creations. Be sure to save your bean water, too, to use as a soup base for a future meal.

BPA BEACHES

Why cook from scratch instead of buying canned? Many food and beverage cans are still lined with bisphenol A (BPA). Scientists have found widespread contamination and high levels of BPA in ocean water and sea sand. Because it mimics the hormone estrogen, this man-made chemical can affect our health in dangerous ways we're

---

just beginning to understand. Researchers have taken samples from more than two hundred sites in twenty countries, especially on the coasts of North America and Southeast Asia. They've detected bisphenol A in each batch of water and sand tested.[4] There are few regulations to protect wildlife from becoming overloaded with the chemical, and there is little information out there advising visitors to avoid the most highly contaminated beaches.

Research on lab animals has shown the ill effects of plastic products leaching into their food. Scientists are finding that items made of plastic can contain chemicals that are neurotoxic and carcinogenic and that have a disruptive effect on the body's hormonal messaging system. BPA leaches into our food through plastic packaging. Think about the white vinegar plastic container, your mustard and mayonnaise, the plastic wrap around your cheese, your tube of toothpaste. And most of your canned foods, too. BPA even comes in high doses on the thermal paper receipts you get at the store, in the paper money you handle every day, and perhaps, also, the water faucet in your kitchen sink, with plastic washers and gaskets. It's even in your house dust!

We've learned from public health articles that we are exposed to BPA through inhalation, ingestion, and dermal contact (receipts, money). Furthermore, Dr. Philippe Grandjean, at Harvard's T. H. Chan School of Public Health, has conducted studies in the Faroe Islands, a fishing community near Iceland and Norway, that have proven there are high levels of persistent organic pollutants (POPs) in the blood and milk of nursing mothers. It's yet another study showing us that the chemical additives to plastics are being ingested by an indigenous community whose diet depends on marine life.[5]

22. **Cat Scratching Post.** Our theory is that your average carpet-remnant cat scratch tree only encourages your fur-ball to scratch up your carpet or upholstery. If you give your cat an actual tree branch to sharpen her nails on, she'll leave your furniture alone. Find the perfect curving fat tree limb with two Y-shaped branches so your kitty can have a few good climbing spots. Attach it to a piece of particle-board by screwing the sawed-off bottom of the limb onto it.

23. **Chrome Cleaner.** Polish chrome in your kitchen by using one part white vinegar to two parts water, applied with a microfiber cloth or sponge.

24. **Flower Arrangements.** Rather than buying flowers, which are often produced far from home, using lots of water, pesticides, and fuel for shipping, pick some of your own and bring them inside to enjoy. Experts estimate it takes nine thousand metric tons of carbon dioxide emissions to get one hundred million roses (the number thought to be given in the United States on Valentine's Day alone) from the flower farms in countries like Ecuador, Kenya, Colombia, and even Norway to your florist. That's the equivalent carbon emissions from all the cars driven for one year in a small American town.[6] If you don't have flowers to pick around your home, fashion a pretty arrangement from other things like branches from flowering trees and shrubs. In the winter, we take branches with buds on them to "force" indoors so they leaf out early. They look spare and beautiful in a large vase. Nothing better than a vase or jar full of something pretty from outdoors to remind you of the natural bounty around us.

25. **Dishwasher Rinse Aid.** Replace your rinse agent with vinegar and you'll get the same results, if not better. Just don't try

this if your dishwasher has rubber parts where the rinse aid goes, as vinegar can corrode rubber. Instead, you can try putting a cup of vinegar in a small cup in the upper shelf of the dishwasher so it can splash out during the wash cycle.

26. **Easter Egg Dye.** Here's an eco-friendly way to dye Easter eggs. Take dried-out, colorful nontoxic markers, put them upside down in glasses of water, add a splash of vinegar, and you have the perfect egg dye. As an added bonus, this will magically revive your markers.

27. **Face Scrub.** As you know from page 15, many store-bought scrubs contain microplastics that are bad for you and bad for the environment. Avoid that unhealthy stuff by making Ottawa resident Andrea Drajewicz's favorite DIY face scrub. Take 1 cup raw rolled oats, 1 cup baking soda, 3–4 tablespoons poppy seeds, and 3–4 tablespoons dried orange peel. Throw it all in the blender and pulse it until the oats and orange peel are largely powdered, and then store it in a mason jar. To use it, mix 1 tablespoon of the powder with a bit of warm water in your hand and massage it onto your face, avoiding the eye area. Wash it off with warm water and do a final splash with cold water. If your skin is dry, mix the scrub with sweet almond oil or a blend of holly and jojoba oil instead of water. If your skin is oily, follow up with a "toner" of witch hazel.

28. **Cling Wrap.** You already know why to avoid the plastic kind. This is Rebecca's tutorial for reusable, waterproof cloth wrap: Start with lightweight woven cotton fabric. Old sheets, button-down shirts, and thin denim pants work perfectly. Cut the fabric into pieces of your desired shapes and sizes. If you have pinking shears, use those to prevent

the edges from fraying; if not, enjoy the fashionably fringed edges you'll get over time. Heat your oven to 150 degrees Fahrenheit, or its lowest setting. Coat a baking tray with parchment paper. Set a piece of your fabric onto the parchment paper. Sprinkle beeswax beads or shavings from pure beeswax candles over the entire surface of the fabric, aiming for full and even coverage. Use less than you think you'll need; it's easy to add more.

Set the tray in the oven for about eight minutes, or until the wax has melted and soaked into the fabric. Remove the tray from the oven as soon as the wax has all melted. If there are areas of fabric that aren't fully coated, just sprinkle on more wax and pop it back into the oven to melt. When the fabric is fully inundated with wax, remove it from the oven and allow it to cool. Use these to cover containers of food you store in the fridge or for potlucks and picnics or to wrap a sandwich, cut fruit, and other foods in packed lunches. Stiff waxed fabric will warm and become more pliant with the heat from your hands. Store them in a warm spot in your kitchen. If the wax wears out, just repeat the process. When they reach the end of their lives, add them to your compost bin.

29. **Floor Cleaner/Shiner.** Wood floors can be mopped and shined with a spritz of 1 teaspoon castile soap in hot water with 10 drops of your favorite essential oil (lemon, grapefruit, lavender, tea tree). Or you can use half a bucket of warm water with ¼ cup vinegar and a few drops of essential oil.

30. **Brown Sugar.** Does your brown sugar turn into a hard block because you don't use it often enough? No need to buy it because you can make fresh brown sugar whenever

you need it. For a cup of light brown sugar, all you need is 1 cup sugar and 1 tablespoon molasses. Mix it all together and you have light brown sugar! For dark brown sugar, you guessed it, you'll need 2 tablespoons molasses to 1 cup white sugar. Done!

31. **Fairy Houses.** Yep, we make 'em, in the woods in secret hollows and in the garden around our local public library, and no store-bought fairy house could ever compare. Only the fairies can find them tucked among the plants. This is a great project to do with kids and adults of all ages. At Liesl's generational family home in New Hampshire, they have a tradition of making fairy art and houses along a forest pathway. Stones, pine cones, leaves, sticks, bark, and even mushrooms are used to create mandala art and fairy villages to delight passersby on their way to the lake. No mortar or nails needed, just build with the natural materials you find—fairy houses aren't meant to last for long.

32. **Laundry Soap for Delicates.** Use dish soap to hand wash your delicates—no need for specialty detergents.

33. **Mayonnaise.** Place ¼ cup light olive oil, 1 large egg, ½ teaspoon mustard powder, and ½ teaspoon salt in a blender or food processor. Mix it well, then *slowly* add 1 cup more of light olive oil as you continue to run the food processor. The slower you pour, the more it emulsifies. Next, slowly add the juice of half a lemon. Store in a glass jar with a tight lid, in the fridge, and this mayo will keep for a couple of weeks.

34. **Sink Scrub.** Scour your sink with baking soda and a sprinkling of lime juice. It's the best cleaner out there.

35. **Soap Dispenser.** Take a mason jar with a wide-mouth lid

and punch a hole in the center of it (we use an old-fashioned can opener to do this) wide enough to fit a reused pump from a bottle of hand soap into it. Use a silicone sealant to lock the pump down to its center hole, and smooth out the sharp edges around the hole.

36. **Toothpaste.** Put 1 cup baking soda into a small mixing bowl, then add 2½ teaspoons fine sea salt, and mix well. Add ¼ teaspoon peppermint oil (or the extracts or oils of your choice). Mix well. Add powdered xylitol or stevia to taste. Adjust as desired. If you've added too much salt, flavoring, or sweetness, add a bit of extra baking soda, taste again, and make any desired changes. Store finished toothpaste in a small jar with a tight lid. This makes enough to fill four 4-ounce mason jelly jars each about three-quarters full.

37. **Nut Butters.** We cut costs by buying nuts in bulk and then grinding them in a high-powered blender to make almond, peanut, cashew, hazelnut, and sunflower butters. (This only works with a high-powered blender or food processor.) Almond flour is also a staple and easy to make in the mixer.

38. **Applesauce.** Because we have apple trees, it's manda-tory to make homemade applesauce. Our recipe is easy and sugar-free. Just cut up the apples, with skins still on. Core them (and save the discards for composting or vinegar). Throw the apple chunks into a big pot and add water to just below the tops of the apples. Add one cinnamon stick. Cover the pot and let it simmer for 25–35 minutes, or until the apples are soft. If you have a slow cooker, it can also make great applesauce. You won't need as much water in the cooker. Follow the same instructions as for a pot, and watch your apples slowly caramelize over time. They will

soften enough for sauce in a few hours. Run the soft apples through your food mill or simply mash them with a fork and you have pure, delicious applesauce! We put the sauce in mason jars and freeze them for the winter.

39. **WD-40:** In a pinch, use any kind of cooking oil to quiet squeaky hinges.

40. **Tarps.** Make your own tarp from woven plastic chicken feed bags. If your city is part of the backyard chicken movement, some of your neighbors will have sturdy chicken feed bags they'd be happy to part with. Cut them open and stitch them together with a sewing machine (fast and easy!), by hand (a great beginner's sewing project, use a big needle and sturdy thread), or duct tape (very fast, if a bit sticky). You can also just cut one feed bag open to make a small tarp for projects. These make great ground covers for camping, mess collectors under art projects or toddler high chairs, mats under pet bowls, or covers for anything you'd like to keep dry.

41. **Fingerless Gloves.** Next time you come across a moth-eaten or otherwise tattered wool sweater that's beyond repair, turn it into hand warmers. First, felt the sweater by washing it in a vigorous, hot water cycle with a squirt of soap or detergent (you can do this by hand or machine; see page 101 for a description of how to felt). Once your felted wool is dry (feel free to toss it in a dryer for extra felting action), cut yourself a pair of fingerless gloves: the end of each sleeve is bound to fit someone's hands, and if you need something bigger, cut two rectangles, each big enough to go around your palm, wrist, and forearm. Stitch each rectangle into a tube, leaving a space along the seam open for your thumb.

42. **Rags.** Just a reminder, folks, a rag is just another word for old threadbare clothes, towels, and bedding—you never need to buy them. Save them all in a rag bag for household use.

43. **Travel Mug Cozies.** Don't throw out your favorite socks when they're past mending or you can't find the mate! Cut off (and recycle with textiles) the foot part and use the remaining tube piece as an instant travel mug cozy. Simply slide it over any mug to keep your beverage warm and your hands comfortable. The cut ends will roll right up, there's no need to hem or stitch or glue anything.

44. **Deodorant.** Mix together two parts softened coconut oil with two parts baking soda and two parts cornstarch. If your coconut oil is stiff, set it in a warm spot to soften; there's no need to melt it. Add a few drops of your favorite essential oil(s). Stir well, then spoon everything into a small, wide-mouth jar or other container. You can store it in the fridge if you'd like a solid bar, or keep it in your bathroom and use your fingers to melt a bit from the jar and spread a thin layer of it onto your armpits or wherever you get sweaty. This deodorant doesn't have the same texture, feel, and behavior as standard stick deodorant, but it really does work.

45. **Chocolate Bark.** This is a favorite activity of ours, especially around the holidays, as it makes a great seasonal, handmade gift. Line a rimmed baking tray with parchment paper or buttered aluminum foil. Prepare the toppings of your choice: we like chopped nuts and dried fruits, spices such as cinnamon and cardamom, fresh or dried lavender or rose petals, and a dash of sea salt. Melt the chocolate of your choice, dark, semisweet, or milk. You can use chips or a bar, whichever chocolate you like best (and if you pick

chocolate produced without the labor of enslaved people, your candy will be even sweeter). You can easily melt
chocolate in a glass bowl in the microwave: heat for thirty
seconds, stir, and repeat just until melted. Pour chocolate
into the lined tray, quickly smooth it out, and immediately
sprinkle it with your chosen toppings. Set the tray in the
fridge until the chocolate is set, then break into bite-size
pieces and store in an airtight container in the fridge (or
just eat it all right away; that works, too).

46. **Cat Toys.** If you don't have baby socks, ask for one in your
    local giving group. Someone is bound to have an odd one
    that's missing its mate. Stuff the baby sock two-thirds full
    with any fabric scraps or other stuffing you have available,
    adding a few pinches of dried catnip, a few strips of crin-
    kly plastic from a chip bag or other snack packaging, and
    a little metal bell if you have one. Tie the end of the sock
    closed with a piece of yarn or string, leaving some of the
    sock unstuffed as a sort of "tail." Give to your cat or make a
    collection of them for your local animal shelter.

47. **Glass Stovetop Cleaner.** This is one of Rebecca's favorite
    cleaning tricks for glass-top stoves. Sprinkle the top of your
    stove with cream of tartar and then pour on a splash of hy-
    drogen peroxide, just enough to form a smooth paste. Use a
    washcloth to rub this paste around the entire stovetop for
    about a minute, then use a clean, damp cloth to remove the
    paste. You can also use baking soda and hydrogen peroxide
    to clean the enameled surfaces of electric and gas stovetops
    (just don't use them on the metal elements). Sparkling!

48. **Shoelaces, Yarn, and Gift Ribbon.** There's no need to
    ever buy a shoelace again. Take a cotton jersey knit T-shirt

that's too worn for wear. Starting at the bottom hem, make an angled cut about one and a half inches up into the shirt. Line up your scissors so that you're cutting a strand of shirt parallel to the hem all around the shirt, keeping your strip about one and a half inches wide. Don't worry if the width wobbles a bit or the edges aren't perfectly clean. Continue this way around and around the T-shirt, stopping to cut your strand free when you hit the sleeves. Carefully work your hands along the entire strip, pulling on the fabric gently, which will cause the knit to roll onto itself, hiding any imperfections in edge or width. Roll this into a ball, and you have T-shirt yarn perfect for shoe- and bootlaces, all-purpose cord or string, gift wrapping "ribbon," and thick crochet or knit items.

49. **Yummy Instant Coffee.** Are you familiar with those special-brand single-use instant espresso/latte/mocha packets that only require the addition of hot water in your mug? We make our own using instant espresso powder, unsweetened cocoa powder or hot chocolate mix, and powdered milk. All of these ingredients are available in bulk or in glass or metal

containers, so if you mix your own ingredients up to taste, you'll skip the single-use plastic packaging and the expense and get a decent cup of joe to boot. Experiment to find the mixture and ratios you like best, then fill a small jar and keep it in your office drawer, car, daily bag, or camping gear.

50. **Book Covers.** When Rebecca's daughter started high school, it came to her attention that "no one" makes textbook covers from paper grocery bags anymore. Rebecca set to work to pass this important skill onto her daughter (while telling her all about how she had to carry her own lead-weight books five miles uphill through the mud each day). If you never learned or don't remember, ask your local librarian or find an online tutorial. This is easy, fast, affordable, customizable with drawings or collage art of your choice, and so much better for our planet than the stretchy synthetic fabric covers in the school supplies aisle of your local big-box store.

We Invite You to Make & Fix

We have three Make and Fix assignments for you. Here's your chance to play with all sorts of fun Rs: Rejuvenate, Remake, Renovate, Rot (as in make compost!), Repair, Refurbish, Reupholster, Restore, Remodel, Repaint, Reconfigure, Re-cover, Redesign, and Rethink.

First up, Make: Choose one thing to Make for yourself. Pick from our list or your own, and Make it. This can be something consumable, like a spice blend or stock, or something durable, like a sock cozy for your travel mug. It can be something simple (turn a large bowl and some smooth stones into a birdbath) or it can be more complicated (turn a free wooden pallet into a coffee table). The key is to make something you want or need, and to check some things off your shopping list by making them yourself. You'll be surprised at how this exercise can get your creative juices flowing.

Next up, Fix. Tackle one task on your list of Things That Don't Quite Work. Again, you can make this as simple or complicated as you desire. Stitch up the inside corner of a coat pocket (Frankenstein stitches are fine, no one will see them), unwobble a chair leg, rewire a broken lamp, make dresser drawers glide again, fix a leaky or drippy faucet, give your HVAC unit an annual maintenance checkup. There are free tutorials online (and possibly in your friends' brain banks) for each of these fixes.

Finally, we ask you to offer to Make or Fix something for someone else. Spread the word that this is how we can get things done, that we are capable of helping ourselves and one another with many of life's repairs, that we can make many of the things on our shopping lists. Find fellow Makers and Fixers in our discussion forum at buynothinggeteverything.com. The more we make our Making and Fixing public, the more we normalize this approach, the less we'll consume, and the more industrious we will be when it comes to life's bigger problems.

STEP 6: SHARE, LEND & BORROW

> "I believe in the power of community to make the world better,
> I believe in neighbors knowing each other, and I believe that
> less reliance upon material goods for our happiness—and more
> upon our relationships—is a healthy way to live."
>
> —*Anastasia McAteer, Ocean Beach, California*[1]

Some of us may think that sharing is the same as giving, but we believe it is a distinctly different act. The Oxford English dictionary provides synonyms for sharing, like *split* and *divide*, with the following definition: "give a portion of (something) to another." In this sense, sharing implies you have excess to give. We're big on sharing, because when we look closely at what we have saved up, especially when we're mindful not to throw things away, we find we have plenty to share with others. So sharing is a two-step act. First, you must create or save up collections of things, and second, you then apportion shares of what you have. In fact, we enjoy purposefully saving up items just to share them, dishing out portions to those who'd like some. We also publicly share things as an example for others to follow, encouraging them to make collections of the things they tend to have a lot of, and then share their bounty when there's plenty to dole out.

Lending and borrowing are a lot more clear-cut than sharing, and we've worked hard to get our neighbors to join us in a unique model of a lending library. Most "libraries of things" that we know about in the United States are set up and run by municipalities or organizations, and are built to follow the traditional public library model: a building is procured, staff are hired, items are purchased and entered into a tracking system, and then locals can visit at set hours to check out items such as ladders, power tools, and plumbing repair kits. These are undeniably helpful and important resources, but we wanted to add a different model of lending to the mix. Many of us have items we want to keep but that we don't use every day, things we'd be happy to loan out if we knew and trusted the borrowers. Before we started our first Buy Nothing group, we ran an experiment on ourselves and invited our community to join us, going through our homes to find objects we'd be happy to loan out to friends or friends of friends. We came up with a huge list: tents, sleeping bags, and all sorts of camping gear; suitcases and other travel items; cloth napkins, tablecloths, serving plates, punch bowls, glasses, deviled egg plates, cake stands, and other dinnerware; fabric bunting, tea party sets, and other party items; picnic baskets and coolers; edgers, mowers, pruners, ladders, and hedge trimmers; tools for auto and home repair; and the list went on. There are so many items we have and find useful when we need them, but they sit in our closets and garages for the majority of every year. What if we each thought of these items as a local resource, a private collection available for loan, and ourselves as the librarian, in full control of borrowing rules, dates, and screening of borrowers? What if we each posted a list of our items and rules to a central site, so everyone could look items up and contact people directly? We wouldn't need a building or staff or funding; we'd be using what we already had, putting everything to use and reducing our collective purchasing by sharing items that can easily be shared without any negative impact on our own use of the items whenever we needed them.

We loved this idea! Most of our community was mystified: Why in the world would we loan valuable items to strangers? What would compel people to care for items and return them? Wouldn't people bring things back broken, or not at all? Our self-run lending library idea fizzled because we hadn't accounted for the most important element of sharing: trust.

It turns out that trust is exactly what grows in local gift economies. Each time a stranger gives a gift or receives one, people who seemed "strange" are suddenly tied together through generosity, and trust is built up. Strangers become acquaintances, then friends, and the idea of loaning your great-aunt Dori's china platter to a friend isn't daunting at all. Yes, things are sometimes damaged, but friends naturally offer to fix or replace what they break, and mistakes are understood and forgiven because the relationship with your friend is more important than a weed whacker's split handle or a chipped plate.

We saw our original personal lending library idea come alive in Buy Nothing Project groups as a wholly normal function of the relationships built among people who give to one another. Giving away something we don't need or want is easy compared to lending something we do, but there is an inborn human desire to care for the people we know and trust. Sharing is a sign of a healthy giving network, and it's at the heart of Buying Nothing.

Create Your Shareocracy

Ben Williams started his project, the Shareocracy of the Future, while working at a Montreal-area farm, where he was paid in produce for his contribution. He found he had plenty of food to eat, from his veg-earnings, that he wanted to be sure to share it with others, rather than tossing it back into the compost pile at the farm. Ben knew the beautiful vegetables could feed the people of Montreal. According to a CBC news story, Ben set up "shop" in a public park,[2] displaying his colorful earnings for all to see: beautiful tapering orange carrots, deep greens like spinach and chard, and boxes overflowing with red cherry tomatoes. At first, people walked by, not sure what his intentions were, but the idea caught on quickly once everyone realized the food was free! Soon people were coming to him regularly for their weekly garden bounty fix.

His experiment was a hit. Ben wrote a kind of manifesto about his project on his Facebook page:

"The idea of a genuine culture of sharing is so simple but goes deep. While seemingly naïve, it addresses many important issues including sustainability, our general sense of community and connection and other negative consequences of the 'endless growth economy.' It's impossible to quantify, but if we grow the genuine culture of sharing, even a little, already we're making kinder, more sustainable communities. At its limit, we could radically change the economy, how we treat the Earth, and how we engage with each other and our communities."

We couldn't agree more with these sentiments. Ben was able to make an impact on people's lives, showing them that it is possible to share freely. His plan is to travel across Canada, staying and working on farms, and continuing his shareocracy experiment to show people that a radical shift away from buying and consuming is possible, in the face of widespread sharing.

The gift economy, and individual acts of giving, promotes reusing, sharing, and lending. This, in turn, also reduces waste. It's time to discover the power of sharing, lending, and borrowing and how it can help you in your Buy Nothing journey. What resources do you have access to that you can share? You might be surprised to find out.

LIESL'S GARDEN GLOVE LOVE

I first noticed the gloves when my kids were learning to ride their bikes, chugging along a little haphazardly and slowly. We kept seeing lost gloves by the side of the road and decided to pick them up. One by one, over the course of a few days, we managed to collect twenty pairs! We're an island of avid gardeners, farmers, and a world-famous garden tour called Bainbridge in Bloom. Twelve months of gardening weather here in Puget Sound affords us four seasons of dirt digging, and too many gloves fallen by the side of the road.

Over the years, we have gathered hundreds of pairs of gloves, plus hundreds more singles waiting for a mate. Rather than let these gloves go to waste, we wash them and send them to Kathmandu to protect the hands of the ragpickers. Life as a ragpicker is tough, and many are children in their preteens. These kids, and plenty of adults, make a living picking through other people's trash to compile enough plastic bags and water bottles to send to India for recycling. It's a decent living, but the conditions are among the worst on the planet.

Most ragpickers have no gloves at all, and some wear just one glove, as that's all they have. They pick barehanded through broken glass and human excrement to find their quarry, and the best protection they can have is on their hands (it doesn't hurt to have a face mask, too). More than two hundred ragpickers work at the city's dump some fifty miles from Kathmandu. Many children pick plastics from the Bagmati River as well as from the streets of Kathmandu. Having a glove or two could save a child from infection, disease, and dysentery that comes with the territory.

And so the glove project was born, or as my son calls it, "Garden Glove Love." Our roadside garden gloves, which would otherwise languish in ditches, have become a resource for people who need basic sanitary protection on the other side of the planet. It doesn't cost anyone anything to just pick them up, and we clean them and then throw them in our duffels and deliver them in person during our trips to Nepal. When the magnitude 7.8 earthquake hit Nepal in 2015, we found that everyone, millions of people, needed work gloves to pick through the rubble.

This is just one example of creative sharing and repurposing. Discarded and lost gloves in one country have found eager hands in another.

Step 6: Share

Now that you're actively Buying Nothing, what have you been doing with all of the time you've found not shopping? We try to replace the time we'd spend shopping with time spent Making, Fixing, and Sharing. This is a way to deepen your Buy Nothing experience and go longer without buying, while also giving back to the community in meaningful ways.

Here are some ways to get you started. There are so many

methods of sharing, and diverse forms of the following ideas exist around the world. Can you create your own spin on them and introduce some of these ideas in your communities?

1. **Host a clothing share.** We don't call them swaps, because frankly, most people have tons of clothes they want to get rid of and only need a few items to make over their wardrobe. *Swap* implies a one-for-one trade, and our idea is to gather people together so they can share freely. Have them bring any clothes they're done with and lay them all out on a table. You can separate them by kind or just let people look through the piles. It's fun to do it in someone's home, or try it on a dry sunny day in a public park. You'll be impressed with all the cool new togs you'll come home with. Some groups have a point person who then takes all of the clothing that is left over and turns it into a round-robin for those who missed the event (see #3).

2. **Start a meal club.** Get a group of culinarily minded friends together and start a meal club. This takes batch cooking to a new level and varies your meals while you use only one recipe in your own kitchen. So, if there are five of you, then you make five lasagnas, for example, and get four other homemade meals in return for your family! If people in your group have freezer space, it's great to do this monthly and choose foods that freeze well. Everyone cooks on the same day (Sunday seems to be the most popular choice), then meets up to swap finished food all at once. Each participant goes home with a stack of entrees for the coming month, whenever they need a home-cooked meal that only takes reheating. It can also be done with fresh foods. Just assign

a day to each person for their bulk cooking. Who doesn't want a break from cooking some nights?

3. **Launch a round-robin.** Round-robins are a collection of items that you send into your community for people to pass around, take what they want, and add to. We often create a collection for specific sizes of children's clothing, for example. But round-robins can be created for women's and men's clothing, makeup, kitchen supplies, and toys.

4. **Create a garden share group.** When Liesl first moved to Bainbridge Island, she started a group called Island Garden Share, where she invited people to come to her house once a month and bring with them perennials, cuttings, and veggie starts from their gardens to share with the group. Each participant would go home with new plants and veggies to put in their gardens. It was a garden plant potluck of sorts and saved everyone so much money in starting new perennial beds. Another added benefit? It was the best way to meet others who shared a passion for growing perennials and vegetables.

5. **Go gleaning.** When it's harvesttime, find apple trees, blackberry bushes, grapevines, pear trees, any fruits or vegetables growing on public land that would otherwise go to waste, pick the produce, and share it with everyone.

6. **Create a "Buy Nothing, Share Freely Holiday Shop."** We've run a free holiday shop for years, a party where people bring items that are gift-worthy and both children and adults can take any item they'd like to give to family members and friends. Everyone goes home with armloads of gifts for the holidays.

7. **Build a Little Free Library.** Little Free Libraries have been a thing for years and they're such a cool gift to give the world. Build a little weatherproof box that can hold books, and put it out at the end of your driveway or other safe location accessible to your neighbors (apartment lobbies are perfect, with permission from your building manager). People will come and take what they like and add to the collection. Visit littlefreelibrary.org for all of the details, including building plans and a global map of Little Free Libraries.

8. **Start a library of things.** Lending libraries are not only for books! We've seen libraries for tools, seeds, housewares, and fancy clothes, all started up as innovative local resources for neighbors to share. Choose an item or items you'd like to steward, like cloth napkins for events (this saves so much on paper waste), metal cutlery, wineglasses, plates, camping gear, snowshoes, carpet steamer, etc., and your neighbors will thank you. Libraries of things are popular municipal resources, and gift economies serve to decentralize them, meaning that each of us can be a steward of an item or items and loan them out, rather than the community managing a space for all that stuff. Choose the item you'd like to loan to people, let everyone know, and be the go-to person for that much-needed thing.

9. **Establish a community free box.** Much like Little Free Libraries, sometimes people just put a weatherproof free box out for passersby to contribute to and take from. Free boxes become gathering places and sources of great stories. Your local dump or transfer station is a great place to have a "free shop" where people can stash their perfectly usable items for reuse as a last resort for things on their way to the landfill.

10. **Create a fleet of "free bikes"** and set them free for people to ride from place to place. We did it, and spray-painted the bikes with a "ride me" sign on them.

11. **Start a Fix-It Fair.** These are so essential! Assembling local engineers, electricians, carpenters, seamstresses, and MacGyvers for a Fix-It Fair can go a long way to prevent things from going into the landfill. You may already have one nearby, so just type "Repair Café" or "Fix-it Fair + [your state or region]" into your browser and see what pops up.

12. **Dream up your adventure, and borrow what you need.** If you want to try snowboarding but don't have a snowboard, just ask to borrow one! When you show others that it's okay to ask, they will follow your lead and do the same. Now people can go paddleboarding, kayaking, skateboarding, and bicycling without having to buy all the equipment. We even started a Facebook group called the Buy Nothing Travelers' Network, where members of the Buy Nothing Project network can connect with members around the world to borrow items when they visit their cities or towns. It also allows them to leave behind items they may have bought but cannot take with them when they travel back home. You can do this on a personal scale by activating your friends-of-friends network to find people to share with whenever you travel.

13. **Start a skills library within your local gift economy or through your social networks.** Ask people what their strengths are, what they'd like to be called upon to help people with, create a list of who can help with what, and let the sharing of skills begin!

14. **Create a Buy Nothing back-to-school initiative.** Encourage your community to pool the typical supplies students

need to return to school. Most households have these things in excess, and some companies will be happy to contribute office supplies like pens, pencils, dividers, folders, scissors, staplers, staples, erasers, index cards, and three-ring binders. If you collect these items throughout the year, you could hold a back-to-school sharing night for families to come and pick up what they need. Buying more of these items, when they are in abundance in our towns, is completely unnecessary.

15. **Start a monthly "Really Really Free Market."** Minneapolis has a successful free market that has benefited many families. You could start one in your city or town, too. Minneapolis's Really Really Free Market, at East Phillips Park, is very popular. People contribute what they no longer need and pick up what they do. Here's what they put out in the local newspaper to spread the word: "Everything here is FREE: offer what you'd like to give and take what you would like to receive. Food, music, and company are as welcome as objects. Enjoy an afternoon in the gift economy! Please treat everything as a gift, and please take back with you any things that you have brought that nobody has taken."

16. **Have a ski/bike/sporting goods swap.** In the winter, you could organize an annual ski swap for families to give away and also receive skis, poles, helmets, snowboards, snowshoes, winter clothing, boots, etc. And in the summer you could do the same for bikes, helmets, in-line skates, skateboards, camping gear, backpacks, kayaks, paddleboards, etc. In the fall, another swap could outfit kids for soccer, lacrosse, football, field hockey, volleyball, and all upcoming organized sports that require uniforms, cleats, etc. Kids outgrow their shoes and clothes so quickly—there's no need to buy new every year!

17. **Be a community fixer.** Are you good at fixing something in particular? If you have a special fixer skill, broadcast it to let everyone know. It's a great way to make instant friends. Debi Baker, a Buy Nothing member in California, loves fixing sewing machines. She acquires old broken ones that people can't be bothered with, fixes them, and then gives them away. We know a few bike mechanics who also love to refurbish bikes to set them free again. Paonia, Colorado, has a wonderful collective of bike geeks who have a passion for teaching others how to repair and maintain bikes. That's a model for any community, waiting to be replicated the world over. Maybe there's some superpower fix-it skill you have that you could share, too.

18. **Host a book-sharing event.** Invite friends to bring books they're finished with, and encourage them to pick one or two out from the communal book pile to take home. And in this spirit, please share this book when you're done with it. We appreciate the irony of our Buy Nothing book being sold. So, please give it, lend it, borrow it, even donate it, and encourage your recipients to share it and write their own sharing ideas in the margins so these ideas can be spread widely and freely.

19. **Have a toy party.** Collect the toys your kids are finished with into a box or basket, and at the next child's birthday party, invite other parents to bring the toys their kids are done with and encourage everyone to shop for new toys!

20. **Garden communally and share produce.** If you have growing space, turn it into a neighborhood garden. Gardening is time-consuming, and plants benefit from daily attention. Sharing the land and work will increase yields, bring-

ing food and joy to more people. You can also contribute your excess produce to a Grow Free cart, a beautiful movement of colorful carts started in Australia where people share their excess produce and take what they need from the carts. Look for a Grow Free cart near you at growfree .org.au, or start a cart for your community. This idea from Down Under deserves to take root around the world.

Still can't think of some way to kick-start sharing in your community? Here's an idea that each one of us can do. We collect a few things that we use to craft special gifts, or give to others who use them regularly, or give to people who would otherwise not have access to these things. We believe each of us can do this. If every one of us became a known steward of a particular item that ends up in landfills, each of our communities would be so much less wasteful.

Here's an example. Our local recycle bins do not accept aluminum foil. So our friend Jane Martin decided to become a foil steward. She put a bucket out in front of her house so people could drop their aluminum foil off there. We'd save it up and give our stashes to her at meetings we attended together. Every few months, she took it all to a scrap metal business that paid her for the aluminum foil! Jane also has a special talent for making jewelry. Throughout the year, Jane collects beads and every kind of jewelry from the community. She has set up six jewelry drop-off sites on the island for people to leave their random single earrings, Grandma's old jewelry, broken strands of beads, or just our own personal stashes of jewelry we've outworn. From that, Jane and her jewelry students craft beautiful works for the women who live in our local domestic violence shelter. The new jewelry is an opportunity for our community to help bring a little bit of beauty back into lives that have been disrupted.

50 Things We Share

We're collectors of many things that each have a purpose in this world. Here are fifty things we share as examples of what anyone could do. What waste stream are you willing to steward? There are so many that can benefit you and your community! (For those of you with hoarding tendencies, think about specializing in just a few things and letting the rest go. Choose your focus items, and then free up the rest by giving them to others who would like them.)

1. **Garden Gloves.** Collect found gloves, just as Liesl does, to share with fellow gardeners or for community work projects.
2. **Sunglasses.** We collect sunglasses, even if they're a little scratched, and Liesl takes them to the Himalayas to give to porters and local villagers who regularly suffer from snow blindness. They're lightweight and easy to transport.
3. **Candles and Candle Wax.** We make lots of candles (see page 147). Big ones. We take people's scrap wax from half-burned candles and upcycle them into new candles. It's easy, fun to do with the kids, and costs us nothing, and they make great gifts. When we don't need more candles for ourselves, a local nonprofit that serves adults with intellectual disabilities collects our wax scraps for their fire-starter business.
4. **Single Socks.** Kids in our local schools collect socks for the homeless, and we've found that even asking for singles

from other families is proving fruitful. The kids match singles together ("That's where they end up! In the neighbors' drawers!") and take them to a nearby homeless shelter. Attractive mismatched socks are shared with friends who love that look.

5. **Bubble Pack Mailer Envelopes**. These are good to stockpile because many individuals and businesses can reuse them, rather than buying new.

6. **Metal Beer and Bottle Caps**. Artists in our community want these. So we save them in a hanging basket in our recycling area, and when the basket is full, it gets dropped off at an artist friend's workplace.

7. **Wine Corks**. These are also saved in a basket and either go to artists (see Pinterest for beautiful DIY creations made with cork) or to the Cork Forest Conservation Alliance's recycle program at our local winery.

CONSERVE YOUR CORK

Cork is a renewable recyclable material. Not only will recycling keep your cork out of landfills, but it can help make it so that cork is transformed into flooring and other cool products, like shoes. Organizations like ReCORK or Cork Forest Conservation Alliance can point you to your nearest recycler. Some supermarkets, wine shops, cafés, and vineyards will take your corks, since they have a partnership with Cork ReHarvest. The cork forests of Portugal are one of the oldest forms of sustainable agroforestry in the world. They've been in production since the thirteenth century, and harvesting the cork does not require cutting down the tree. Buying wines that use natural instead of plastic corks helps sustain these forests and their biodiverse habitats that need continued protection. But how do you know which wines have natural corks? There's an app for that! We love this app, put out by ReCORK, called CORKwatch. Do a search for your favorite wine and see what you learn. Kendall-Jackson, for example, has a reserve chardonnay in natural cork, yet their less expensive everyday chardonnay uses plastic. To make it even easier to spot natural wines, Cork Forest Conservation Alliance has a method of identification on the bottles themselves that some wineries are using: if you see an acorn on the bottle, it means the cork is natural.

8. **Children's Books.** For years, we've collected children's books to take to the six Magic Yeti Children's Libraries Liesl's family established in Nepal.

9. **Styrofoam Meat and Fish Trays.** Artists and teachers love flat Styrofoam because it can be used to carve designs for printmaking. Wash, dry, and save these so you can share them with schools, museums, summer camps, and youth groups. We share ours with our local art museum, which uses them regularly for printmaking classes. Katherine Parsons of Virginia, a member of the Buy Nothing Global Team, shares them, too: "I'm no longer afraid to say, 'Hi there!' to a teacher at an art school and ask, 'Can you use these plastic trays I get with my favorite quick dinner from the grocery store?' Items that were dropped in a recycling bin or trash before now become reused over and over."

10. **School Supplies.** Start a school supplies cache to share with your teachers. Ask the teachers what supplies they buy and

use regularly that you could simply collect for them, such as pencils, pens, crayons, colored pencils, three-ring binders, scissors, Magic Markers, rubber bands, pushpins, and stickers. Some community members stockpile these standard school supplies and then share them with families at the beginning of the school year. On the south end of Bainbridge Island, a shed holds school supplies that families share with one another in late August so that no one has to buy them. Everyone contributes.

11. **Flowers.** Share your cut flowers from your garden. Everyone loves fresh flowers.

12. **Stuffed Animals.** There are a number of new lives to be had for stuffed animals: check with your local senior centers, memory wards, childcare centers, animal shelters, artists, and doctors' offices, and you're almost guaranteed to find new homes for your stuffies.

13. **Games.** Same as above. Our state senator, Christine Rolfes, keeps a steadily refreshed collection of Buy Nothing games and toys in a basket outside her office for kids who accompany their parents to the state capitol to meet with her. She's a wonderful role model for her constituents.

14. **Glass Jars.** If you stockpile them and get the word out, someone will likely want them for a project.

15. **Plastic Bottle Caps.** There are some programs out there that will take them or artists who use them.

16. **Jewelry and Beads.** We have a few drop boxes in our town for jewelry and beads for the women's shelter jewelry project our friend Jane Martin created. They even take broken pieces and single earrings. The jewelry is cleaned, sorted, fixed, remade, packaged, and then given to women in the shelter.

17. **Hangers.** Everyone can use hangers, whether they're plastic, wooden, or metal, so be sure to share them rather than throwing them away. Our local dry cleaning business is usually happy to take the metal ones.

18. **Wooden Pallets.** These are popular! If you ever end up with pallets from a delivery, don't trash them, share them. We've made playhouses out of them, and others have used them for fencing, art projects, garden projects, furniture, and hundreds of other things.

19. **Cameras, Video Cameras, and Camcorders.** These are great for film and photography students. Local schools are also always happy to receive photography and film equipment.

20. **Seeds.** In our community, there are a few options for seed sharing. Informally, people get together in the winter, when nothing's really happening in our gardens except kale, and we share seeds. Some of us collect and save the seeds we've harvested and dried during the growing season; others share packets of seeds we know we'll never grow. Our regional public library has a seed library where anyone can contribute and receive seeds, too. The seed packets fit perfectly into old wooden card catalog drawers.

21. **Bubble Wrap.** We save every scrap of bubble wrap for local artists and businesses who would otherwise go out and buy the very same bubble wrap we'd be throwing away. Just stockpile the wrap you accumulate and then find someone who would love to Reuse it. People who are moving will be grateful for it.

22. **Boxes.** On our home island, the Reuse ethic is so strong, there's an online group dedicated solely to sharing moving supplies like boxes, bubble wrap, air packs, packing

peanuts, and paper for wrapping fragile items. We have a big yearly turnover of families moving on and off the island, young families arriving to avail themselves of the great schools, and retirees moving out when their kids have flown the coop. Don't throw away moving and packing supplies—someone nearby can use them!

23. **Broken Ceramics and Glass.** Mosaic artists would love your broken ceramics and glass for their projects.

24. **House Paints, Stains, and Oil.** When we're done with a painting project, we know we can always share the leftovers with anyone embarking on their own home projects.

25. **Plastic Flowerpots.** Some of the farmers at our farmers' market love to get our four-inch pots. Some nurseries will also take unwanted pots.

26. **Art Supplies.** Paints, paintbrushes, glitter, stamps, ink, and glue are always welcome in classrooms, day care centers, senior centers, and our children's museum.

27. **Newspaper.** We know a woman who regularly needs newspaper to start her winter fires. Be sure to ask around to see if anyone could use newspaper for fire starters, gardening, art projects, or puppy training.

28. **Leaves.** Backyard chicken coops get nasty in the wet winter months, so we're always in need of extra leaves that can be thrown in there by the pitchfork full. Throughout the summer, our dried fall leaves act as mulch for the garden, reducing the amount of watering we need to do. Ask before you toss your leaves—a neighbor with animals or plants may need them.

29. **Sticks.** We met each other over sticks—Rebecca once offered up, in a Freecycle group, her beautiful curly willow sticks

from the tree in her backyard, and Liesl was intrigued. Anyone who was bold enough to give away sticks was someone to meet. And here we are now, writing a book together. So you never know whom the weird things that you share could possibly connect you to, and what they might inspire you to do in the future.

30. **Silica Gel.** Silica gel is one of those little-understood materials. Although the packets read "Do not eat, throw away," that doesn't mean they are poisonous. You've likely unknowingly put some in your mouth already or rubbed it all over your body, as it's used in some toothpastes and exfoliants. Silica gel is a nontoxic inert desiccant, and it will dry out anything it sits near. Its uses are many, and hence it's worth thinking twice about throwing the little packets away. We collect them and share them every six to twelve months with artists and others who understand their versatility. Here are just a few of our fave cool uses for these handy packets: Put them in with your silverware. It slows down the tarnishing process. Place them inside your camera cases, with lenses, to keep your equipment dry. Put silica gel in with your boxes of stored photos and slides to preserve them longer. Your down jackets and down sleeping bags will benefit from a few packets of silica gel to keep moisture out. Put a few packets in with your garden seeds to keep them dry. And throw some in with your bulk dry laundry detergent so it doesn't clump up. It works!

31. **SCOBY for Kombucha:** A SCOBY is the gift that keeps replicating itself over and over. It's the stuff of kombucha making that's absolutely necessary for the bubbly goodness. The SCOBY is the "mother" that helps ferment tea and sugar

into kombucha. It's alive and keeps growing with every new batch you make, so giving away your excess SCOBY is a way of life for kombucha makers. Liesl's ever-growing SCOBY has helped cultivate a dozen families' kombucha-making habits.

32. **Clothing.** There are endless ways to share clothing—just see all of our suggestions for clothing parties and round-robins. Clothing is one of the easiest things to share because we all wear it and kids outgrow it so quickly!

33. **Garden.** Share your garden? Sure! There are several ways to do it. You can invite a friend to join you in gardening one season by sharing your plot with them, which means you share in the upkeep, too. That can ease the burden a bit. Sarah Steinberg of Oregon shares her garden another way. Here's how she goes about it: "We grow our fruit, veggie, and herb garden in our front yard and encourage our neighbors to visit it if they need something for dinner or just a snack as they pass. My preschooler in particular loves it when he can show a neighbor where the ripe fruit is."

34. **Perishables.** Have you ever left home for a couple of weeks and still had some perishables in the fridge that could be consumed by someone else? Barb Short of Key Largo shares hers: "When we are going to be away for several days, I give a neighbor the produce/spoilables that won't last the duration for them to use. I share BOGOs [buy one, get ones] similarly since we're just a couple and I don't need twenty-five-pound bags of potatoes. . . . The neighbors always return these little favors or give me plants from their garden that I don't have in my garden."

35. **Dinner.** Double your dinner recipe and share it with some-

one else. Natale Rochlin of Seattle shares meals: "I often double my recipes and provide dinner for my neighbor, a mom and her son. She cooks for me and my family often, too! It's so fun to eat someone else's cooking, but more so [on] those nights when you get a surprise dinner when you really didn't feel like cooking or have anything ready."

Kären Ahern of Bainbridge Island takes this one step further. She not only shares food but encourages others to share it, too, sort of like planting seeds of sharing: "I had fun last Saturday before I left town giving a neighbor a half gallon of coleslaw I made the night before. I asked that neighbor to please share with another she does not know well and for that neighbor to please give some to the folks across the street she had not met. They all got yummy coleslaw with their dinners, but the best outcome was two neighbors across the street from each other finally met after three years! It does take a village, and food sharing is magic."

36. **Books.** Liesl has a guesthouse she rents out as an Airbnb, and inside she has a Little Free Library in a basket for her guests to take books they love and to leave behind ones they're done with. Or find your nearest Little Free Libraries (see page 178) and put your books in them to let others enjoy them, too. You can also go freestyle; Rebecca likes to leave books where they'll be fun surprises for strangers, with a note inside that reads "Yes, this is a free book just for you if you'd like it."

37. **Fabric Scraps.** There's always someone who could use these, like quilters, who love to receive fabric scraps for handmade patchwork quilts. Art teachers and preschool teachers also love fabric scraps for multimedia collages.

38. **Towels and Bedding.** Our wildlife shelter will take towels and bedding in any shape, whether they have rips or stains on them or not. Many pet shelters are happy to receive these items, too.

39. **Chip Bags.** In the UK they're called crisp packets, but whatever name you know them by, they almost all have the same silvery interior, which can make for excellent gift bags. Turning them into shiny gift bags is easy to do: Turn your chip bag inside out, and wash it with dish soap to get rid of any grease. Dry it out. Then Reuse the silvery side as a Mylar-style gift bag.

40. **Milk Cartons.** Pinterest has tons of ideas about how to reuse just about any item out there. Innovative builders are using milk cartons as part of their wall insulation for new homes and structures.

41. **Tiny Toys, Marbles, and Bling.** We keep a mason jar in the pantry where we keep found objects like tiny figurines, matchbox cars, finger puppets, small toys and their parts that we know kids would love to receive as "rewards" from their teachers at school. When the jar is full, we drop it off with our favorite elementary school teachers. Rebecca carries a few marbles in her purse and hides them at adult height around town to brighten someone's day, honoring a memorial service request from her late friend Emily.

42. **Magazines.** When you have a stockpile of your favorite magazines, share them. Our public library has a program where they'll take your magazines and put them in the lobby for others to pick up for a quarter. Proceeds help keep the library running.

43. **Toiletries.** We always save the toiletries we've somehow

acquired but will never use, and then pass them along to our nearby women's shelter.

44. **Dairy Tubs.** Plastic yogurt or butter tubs are something teachers ask for quite often, for STEM science projects. You can save them up in a stack and see if your community might be able to use them.

45. **Reusable Cloth Bags.** (See page 99 for how to make them.) Drop these off at your local food bank. Patrons will appreciate having a reusable bag for their produce.

46. **Medicine Bottles (Amber Prescription Pill Bottles).** People do all kinds of things with these plastic bottles, like use them to store waterproof matches for camping, as a mini sewing kit, to hold the earbuds you keep in your backpack or purse, or for repurposing into herb and spice bottles. Some people will ask for them in your local gift economy. Be sure to stockpile yours and then offer them up when you have enough available for a project.

47. **Bicycles.** Bicycles never need to be thrown away. Even when they are broken beyond repair, they can be used for parts. Check with your local bike clubs and bike shops, as there's usually some bike tinkerer who would love to mine your old bike for parts or refurbish it altogether.

48. **Bike Inner Tubes.** Have you ever seen a bike tube wallet, purse, or belt? Save your inner tubes and give them to a nearby crafter who can Reuse them.

49. **Tarps.** We always keep spare tarps on hand for myriad uses. At home, we use them for all sorts of things during the nine months of rain our island usually slogs through. We like having them on hand to loan. We've lent tarps to neighbors who've had trees fall on their homes and cars,

and we've sent many on their way to communities farther away (these we don't expect to get back; they're on permanent loan) to help people recovering from landslides, earthquakes, and hurricanes. Tarps are among the first material things people ask for when they've lost their homes and belongings so that they can provide shelter either for themselves or for the first few things they start to acquire just after the disaster.

50. **Eyeglasses.** These never need to be thrown away. Save the ones you no longer need and take them to your nearest eye doctor. They'll know where eyeglasses are most needed. Liesl takes the nonprescription one- and two-power generics to share with people in Nepal who don't have access to eye care.

This list isn't exhaustive, but it sheds light on how these consumables can be diverted away from landfills and Reused by people, nonprofits, and companies in innovative ways. Collectively, we're saving these individuals and organizations from having to buy these materials new while at the same time preventing the materials from entering our solid-waste streams. Reducing and Reusing always trumps Recycling.

Reducing and Reusing always trumps Recycling.

What else can we do to share more and help people Buy Nothing? We can lend and borrow, temporarily sharing our stuff with friends and neighbors so that they don't have to buy it new and store it in their already overstuffed homes. Think about the things we have in our garages and closets, on shelves, that are unused most of the year. They're items that we loan out more than once, a durable library of things (and gifts of self) that can be loaned multiple times, saving us money, space, and natural resources.

50 Things We Lend & Borrow

1. **Classroom Snack and Party Supplies.** For each classroom in your local elementary school, start a zero-waste library of things that includes reusable utensils, plates, cups, and cloth napkins. We store a classroom's worth of these supplies in a five-gallon bucket. Everything can be Reused if someone brings the bucket home to wash the items after each use. This saves parents from sending in single-use supplies for class parties and offers kids the lesson of stewardship of shared resources along with their birthday cupcakes.

2. **Coffee Mugs.** You could be the community coffee klatch promoter! Our island community has no lack of coffee mugs. Women's groups, the Rotary Club, and all kinds of organizations have their set of fifty-plus mugs so that everyone can stay properly caffeinated during meetings. Or start a free travel mug program at your local coffee shops so that no one ever has to use a disposable cup.

3. **Kid-Party Supplies.** Party hats, streamers, and party favors are always good to pass on to others who will be throwing a child's birthday party in the near future. We've shared and Reused plenty of party supplies when our children were young, and no one even noticed.

4. **Tents and Camping Equipment.** Liesl's husband works for the North Face, so their family comes by tents easily and is happy to loan them out to campers who don't have their own equipment. These lucky tents spend most of the summer on adventures with different families exploring the Pacific Northwest. Stoves, sleeping bags, pads, tarps, bungee cords, bear-safe food containers: loan out whatever you've got to would-be adventurers. These items are also useful during power outages, storms, and other trying times. What do you have access to through your job that you can share? Books? Food? Scrap lumber?

5. **Snowshoes, Snowboards, Skates, Skis, and Special-Activity Clothing and Gear.** Not everyone needs to buy their own set, and loaning can save a friend the cost of renting. When Liesl's kids outgrew their smaller snowshoes, they kept them to be used as loaners for families who want to head out into the Olympic Mountains to do some exploring. Rebecca's wetsuit from her kayak-guiding days has seen years of use by friends who are heading into the chilly local waters for boating, diving, and surfing. What do you have taking up space in your closet that might be put to good use for someone else? A snowsuit? Diving gear?

6. **Duffel Bags and Luggage.** Liesl loans unused duffel bags to college students moving into their dorm room at the beginning of the school term. Luggage just sits unused between trips—share it in your community, and it can travel the world usefully instead of taking up space.

7. **Sewing Machines.** Rebecca has a simple portable sewing machine that she loans out for quick sewing repairs. This keeps the machine running well (they're happier when they

don't sit unused, getting gummed up with dust), and it keeps clothing mended and in use throughout the community.

GOATS & BEES

You can share just about anything, including goats, if you get creative. Yes, goats! We know people who loan their goats out to neighbors to help clear brambles and invasive species. The goats get free food, and gardeners get free help clearing difficult plants. We also know beekeepers who place their hives in local community gardens and public orchards. The bees are fed by the nectar and pollen in the garden, helping them produce more honey, and gardens and orchards are pollinated, improving food yields.

---

8. **Medical Equipment: Crutches, Foot Braces, Walking Boots, Wheelchairs, Canes, Bath Chairs, Knee Scooters.** All this medical equipment is available in our community for free, passed around from household to household, lightening the burden of traumatic events.

9. **Plumbing Snake.** A plumbing snake is needed in every gift economy to make the rounds from home to home, cleaning hair and whatnot from our pipes.

10. **Public Toy Stations.** Draw inspiration from the collections of beach toys and games available from public self-service stands on the beaches of Tel Aviv. Build a container for toys at your local public park, beach, or other fun location and seed it with toys you'd like others to enjoy. Check in periodically to keep things tidy and to add new toys you've received from friends and neighbors.

11. **Business Attire.** We're seeing this more and more: people are ready to loan out their nice suits, shoes, ties, whatever you may need for that job interview.

12. **Shop Vac and Wet Vac.** These workhorses can be out on loan a few days out of the year and you'll never miss them.

13. **Carpet Steamer and Floor Steamer.** When someone offered a carpet steamer up for givesies in our town, everyone wanted to try it at home. So it got thrown into our lending library, stewarded by Debbie Fecher Gramstad, a long-term member of our own local gift economy who kept track of all the parts and the loan-out list for this great piece of equipment.

14. **Binoculars.** Going on a trip? Ask to borrow some binos. They can be pricey, but if cared for they can be used over and over by many pairs of eyes.

15. **Books.** You probably already do this, loaning out books you've finished. Up your game by hosting a monthly Books-n-Beverages shindig at your favorite local café or pub. Post a flyer inviting people to join you with a couple of books to give away; everyone takes care of their own beverage purchase, but the books and conversation are free for all. And nothing comes close to the cool factor of the original book lender, your local public library; remember to check there first when you're looking for new reads.

16. **Durable School Supplies.** Calculators, protractors, rulers, hole punches, and other long-lived school supplies can be pooled together each summer and distributed again in the fall as they are needed.

17. **Slightly Outdated Entertainment Tech.** Have a CD player, VHS player, cassette player, record player, eight-track, or phonograph? Loan it out! You'll get to meet all your local

hipsters and impress them with your tales of life back before streaming digital content existed. When one person stewards an old VCR or record player for the community, then we all get to listen to our LPs and watch our old home movies from time to time.

18. **Printers and Shredders.** Imagine a community printer and sharing the emotional labor and expense of keeping track of ink cartridges and paper! The shredder is another item that could be shared from home office to home office.

19. **Glasses.** For her wedding about twenty years ago, Rebecca bought two hundred small glasses that work equally well for water, wine, whiskey, and juice, and she's been loaning them out for events ever since. The glasses are stored in their original cardboard boxes, reinforced over the years with packing tape, stacked inside two large plastic tubs. A piece of duct tape on each tub reminds borrowers where to return them after each event. A few glasses are lost at big events, but not as many as you might think. When people borrow directly from an individual, they tend to treat things with great care. This collection of glasses that's been shared for countless weddings, meetings, church, civic, and family functions has even outlasted, well, Rebecca's own marriage.

20. **Dishes, Serving Ware, and Cake Stands.** How often do you really entertain for big groups? Create a set of serving ware to loan out. If your neighborhood has more than one set of dishes to loan, you can even use them for weddings or public events. For years, Rebecca has lent her set of simple white dishes, and she hasn't lost one yet. There is even an area "dish bank" that includes sets of dishes to gift to refugee families who need them when they arrive in the Seattle area.

The same concept applies to serving ware—don't hesitate to loan out your large platters and cake stands. As a bonus, you may get some new recipes to try when they are returned!

21. **Cloth Napkins.** Rebecca has been collecting cotton napkins in an eclectic mix of colors and patterns for more than ten years now. They live in a rolling suitcase that's easy for people to borrow and take to events. So far, they've been at weddings, church suppers, bar and bat mitzvahs, memorial services, school parties, and all sorts of public zero-waste events. Some islanders even have favorites they like to find each time they participate in an event with this shared collection. We think everyone prefers the feel of cloth over paper!

22. **Flatware.** It's easy to put enough flatware for at least twenty-four people into a simple caddy, then set that out for loan along with your lending dishes and other meal supplies. Liesl's and Rebecca's collections have gone to parties at the beach and in the mountains as well as to plenty of potlucks closer to home.

23. **Picnic Basket Set.** This is another easy thing to loan out and share with neighbors.

24. **Tablecloths.** Rebecca's collection of colorful tablecloths has been borrowed for all sorts of events, from informational expos at city hall to community P-Patch garden harvest parties to school sports dinners, weddings, church retreats, and group camping trips. Liesl's linen tablecloths, handed down from her grandmother, are added to the community linen collection when a neighbor's wedding is imminent.

25. **Tea Sets.** Rebecca's daughters love tea, and they are happy to loan out their tea sets, a hit for birthday parties, teddy bear picnics, or bridal and baby showers.

26. **Festive Cloth Bunting.** (See our tutorial to make your own on page 119.) This bunting dates back to the days when we were first experimenting with plastic-free living and replaced balloons with this festive bunting. String them along fences and between trees outside, or along walls and tables inside.

27. **Coolers.** These are easy to loan out between uses for various things—fishing trips, camping expeditions, sporting events, fun runs, road trips, and the like.

28. **Ice Cream Maker.** Every kid should be invited to crank out a batch of ice cream by hand at least once, and you can help them achieve this childhood milestone when you loan out that ice cream maker you use only a few times each summer.

29. **Lawn Mowers and Large Garden Tools and Machines.** If you live in a land of lawns, band together with a neighbor or two and share a mower. The same concept applies to leaf blowers, weed whackers, snowblowers, pressure washers, shovels of all sorts, awls, pitchforks, rototillers, edgers, rakes—anything you need to mow your lawn, garden, or plow.

30. **Tools.** These are great to have in a lending library. Whether someone nearby wants to change a wiper blade or a headlight or tackle something more involved, if you have the tools they'll need, why wouldn't you share them?

31. **Dryer Vent Cleaner.** Our friend Molly is famous on our island for her traveling dryer vent cleaner. Molly is a one-woman fire safety awareness and action force, and thanks to her active pursuit of people, almost everyone Molly knows has a clean, safe dryer vent.

32. **Punch Bowl and Glasses.** This retro party set is fun for parties, but used infrequently, making it ideal for loaning and borrowing.

33. **Lighting of All Kinds.** Those strands of holiday lights sitting in a box would brighten up a neighbor's summer wedding or a local school dance. Twinkly lights are fun all year, and we've noticed that strands of light tend to last longer when they're in use; something about being stored for months, even coiled carefully, does not agree with their wiring. Likewise, extra lamps, flashlights, hurricane lanterns, and candles can all be loaned out for a wide variety of events, from parties to power outages.

34. **Pet Carriers and Pet Grooming and Health Supplies.** Pet carriers are easily shared. Have a leftover cone of shame? Don't be stingy, let Rover next door wear it. The same goes for grooming clippers and nail clippers if you have them. No one's fur grows so quickly that they need a trim every day; loan them out between poodle cuts.

35. **Portable Play Yards, Bassinets, and Other Big Baby Items.** Car seats (not expired, of course), portable playpens and beds, high chairs, and play stations can be so useful when you travel, but they're tough to bring with you. If you have one of these that your baby has outgrown, turn it into a community asset. Grandparents with visiting grandbabies would love to borrow it for family visits, and new parents would love to borrow it for extended use. Rebecca's daughters slept in a portable wooden cradle known as "the island cradle" that kept several generations of island babies safe while they slept—each baby's name was painted onto the bottom of the cradle before it was passed along, creating a

neighborhood heirloom that strengthens ties among people across time.

36. **Inflatable Guest Bed.** This is a great item to loan out, and Liesl keeps one ready for neighbors to use. Even if you use yours every November when your brother comes to visit, you can loan it out the rest of the year.

37. **Formal and Party Clothes.** Can't bear to part with that special formal or cocktail dress, but it's just taking up space in your closet? Invite friends over to "shop" in your closet and borrow some of your favorites for their events.

38. **Tiaras and Jewelry.** There are more occasions than one might think at which a tiara is useful. Rebecca used to make them for a living; now she loans them out to friends of all genders for their own regal use. No tiaras? Maybe you have other jewelry items that add a touch of glamour to life—loan them out and watch happiness increase.

39. **Telescope.** Maybe you use it a few times a year. Let others try it out when you don't need it.

40. **Bullhorns and Protest Signs.** Useful for so many things, but not an everyday item for most of us. If you have one, make it known and lend it out to help others raise their voices to be heard. Rebecca has been collecting the best protest signs left behind after a variety of protests and rallies for some years now. People have fun picking through them for their favorites, and it means it's possible to be ready for a quick bit of democracy in action right away, no need to search for poster board and pens.

41. **Costume Supplies for Adults and Kids.** There are several sets of costumes traveling around the island, and our friend Kate has added her amazing homemade creations (the ba-

nana and the baby pita bread are crowd favorites). If you have a favorite you can't bear to part with, loan it out.

42. **Large Drink Carafes.** Rebecca's mother has a set of heavy glass beverage carafes with handy spigots, and if you promise to return them clean, she'll let you use them at your next party, and she might even give you her famous punch recipe.

43. **Folding Tables and Chairs.** These are bulky to store, but handy to have for various purposes. If you're lucky enough to have the space, make yours available to others who don't.

44. **Pop-Up Canopy.** If you have one of these to lend, your generosity will be greatly appreciated by local nonprofits, sports teams, vendors, wedding hosts, and others looking for sun or rain protection for short events.

45. **Wheels.** Loan out your bicycle so the couple across the street can take their visitors out for a ride, so that the teen down the street can get to and from work or school, or just so someone else can experience the magic of flying on two wheels. We've both borrowed cars when our own were broken down, and loaned ours out when they're running. This kind of loan can be a lifesaver in times of crisis.

46. **Your Expertise.** Share and lend your talents. Can you navigate simple taxes and other government forms? Could you help a new arrival in town learn about community resources, schools, and all the best places for their daily errands? Or do you know how to raise chickens or kids, cook or bake, or create websites? If you know how to do it and it makes you happy, share your knowledge.

47. **Your Elbow Grease.** Offer your help cleaning gutters, shoveling snow, fixing front doors, walking dogs, and otherwise

pitching in. Simple acts of service will nurture a culture of active compassion around you.

48. **Your Company.** Give your companionship during walks, for conversation and coffee, or for card and board games. Start with someone you trust and would like to know better, perhaps a local senior citizen, or someone who always eats lunch alone at work. Even introverts can be lured to make new connections this way.

49. **Space.** Many of us have "third places" in our communities, from coffee shops to formally shared office and meeting spaces. We can extend this trend into our private spaces, too. Get creative and think about what and how you'd like to share your personal space. Rebecca's parents loaned space in their driveway to a family that had moved into an RV when they lost their home. Liesl and her husband offered a final resting spot in their woods to a woman who lost her dog and had no room to bury him near her apartment.

50. **Your Public Presence.** We've seen people in local gift economies offer and ask for intangible gifts of presence, including public support during divorce and protection order hearings, high school reunions, memorial services, and as their plus-one at weddings or concerts.

We Invite You to Share, Lend & Borrow

Make a list of things you own that you could loan out to others. For many, this can be a tough exercise and one that asks us to explore our trust in others, as you may fear that someone will break, or make off with, your stuff. Start by lending something you don't have a deep attachment to, something you don't *need* at home, and offer it to people you know. As you gain firsthand trust in the fact that the majority of people are careful and respectful borrowers, you can branch out. Loan to friends of friends and then to your wider community. Here are the basic ground rules we suggest as you become a lender and borrower:

Lenders—You are in charge of setting all the rules for your own items. You can decide how long to loan them, to whom you're comfortable loaning them, and any rules for use (indoors only, no homes with pets, etc.). If for any reason you're not comfortable lending something to a particular individual or for a particular use, just say so. A simple "I'm taking a break from lending this out" suffices.

Borrowers—Follow all directions and rules set by lenders, and treat things as you would if they were your own treasured belongings. If you break or lose something, fess up, apologize, and ask how you can make it right.

Now, go forth and share! Connect with the buynothingget everything.com discussion forum to dream up your own share-ocracy, where bounty from each of your collections of excess stuff (like corks and padded envelopes) is shared and a library of things (like dishes and home-repair tools) is created so everyone can both lend and borrow. Create a list of the items, and people can just put their name beside the items they loan out with the date and their phone number. Let neighbors know that you'd love to organize a library of things. See where it takes you!

STEP 7: GRATITUDE

Step 7: Gratitude

In addition to giving and asking, expressing gratitude is an essential part of Buying Nothing. Gratitude abounds throughout the Buy Nothing Project. We love seeing "gratitude posts" from members who are grateful for the new toys, clothes, kitchen equipment, or other thoughtful items and services they've received from their neighbors and newfound friends. Without these public displays of thanksgiving, gift giving happens in a vacuum—expressions of appreciation make everyone feel good and connected to the movement.

Gratitude is an important emotion to cultivate. Studies show that giving thanks can actually make you happier. Harvard Medical School's emailed newsletter, *Healthbeat*, notes that "In positive psychology research, gratitude is strongly and consistently associated with greater happiness. Gratitude helps people feel more positive emotions, relish good experiences, improve their health, deal with adversity, and build strong relationships."[1] As more research is published about this natural antidepressant, we're learning that a regular gratitude practice can train our brains to retain more positive thoughts and deflect negative ones, a secret to living longer and more resilient lives. In fact, making a gratitude list (writing down the things you're grateful for) is known to boost your serotonin levels, a chemical found in the brain that contributes to well-being and happiness. These feel-good vibes have myriad benefits to us, including helping us sleep better, reducing inflammation, reducing signs of depression, and aiding us in feeling more satisfied with our lives in general.

We're advocating for the even more powerful practice of expressing gratitude in front of others. These public displays of gratefulness give others a serotonin boost, too. They feel joy vicariously. Gratitude also helps you see that you're part of something much bigger than you, that your happiness is tied to others and our interconnectedness. In a gift economy, gratitude is the sticky honey-like sweetness that binds people closer together, encouraging participants to continue sharing. Without gratitude, we feel as though we're taking part in impersonal transactions, a world where givers give, takers receive, and no one talks about it. Gratitude is a gift of kindness and joy that brings heart and soul to gift economies, strengthening the bonds of community and support.

Without gratitude, and someone taking the time to share it, we would never have heard the story of the little girl in Massachusetts who wrote a Mother's Day card to her mom thanking her for the "surprise toys" she gets "from different people's houses," or the gratitude expressed to the woman in Tucker, Georgia, who invites people to come pick flowers in her garden for Mother's Day. Gratitude gives us a window into the lives going on around us, like that of the woman who expressed her gratitude when her stepfather took a few days off from hiking the Appalachian Trail to visit her, so she asked to borrow, and received, a blender for him because he was "dying for smoothies." These are the stories that bring us together and bind us through the common, yet simple, act of sharing more.

A gift economy is a forum for people to express some form of gratitude for the changes that Buying Nothing has brought about in our lives. And by speaking up about the good that has come your own way, you'll inspire yourself and others to give, to ask, and to share *more*; in other words, to magnify the good. When people see that freely giving, receiving, and sharing has a concrete, meaningful impact on others, they want in on the action. Giving cultures have the power to rekindle hope, raising a flicker of possibility, so long as we aren't afraid to ask for what we truly want. Sharing your gratitude for what you've received, tangible and intangible, can set up human connections that translate into future gifts and loans that can make long-simmering dreams come true, for yourself and for others in your communities.

The Ultimate Gift

Sylvia's story is by far our favorite example of a gift that came to fruition for a couple that had a dream. Despite the pain they felt as their dream dwindled into loss, Sylvia and her wife kept on giving. She shared the truth of her story with her neighbors in a gratitude post (names and some identifying details in this story have been changed).

"I have a gratitude post that will never have the right words to express the gratitude that my wife and I feel. So bear with me here. A bit ago Lucy put an ask out for newborn items for a friend of hers. We, like so many of us in our community, answered the ask.

"When she came to pick up the items, we got to talking about why we had so many baby items but no kids. We talked about our thirteen miscarriages, the foster kiddos that were going to be adoptable that we helped get back home instead, the heartache and the joy of all of it. Standing in my front yard, Lucy said that she thought the parents of the little girl were actually contemplating adoption for her path in life. She offered to ask them if they'd like to meet us. We said of course.

"On Friday, they came. Sitting on my couch, her parents made the ultimate gift offering. They fulfilled the ask of a lifetime. Yesterday morning at 0821 hours, we watched as our gift was born. We took her home this evening.

"I have seen other groups have houses gifted. Cars. A cup of sugar. A lawn mower to borrow (a frequent ask of mine!). I've seen relationships form (my first ask ever was for friends after moving here). I've seen the worst of what group mentality can do. I've seen the best of what a community can accomplish together. I frequently have told people how the BN project has changed my life in so many ways. I just never thought that this would be one of them.

"Tonight we placed our new daughter in an outfit gifted by a member of this group, wrapped her in a blanket gifted by another, buckled her into a car seat that three other BN families have used, strolled her out in a stroller that five BN children have strolled in, drove home, and then placed her to sleep in her BN bassinet. Every item in her bedroom, including the small TV and every piece of clothing in the dressers (and the dressers!) were gifts from Buy Nothing. She has a BN "aunt" (the first person to answer my first ask for friends) and BN "aunt" Lucy.

"Above everything, she has the power of kindness and community surrounding her because of this little project started a few years back. The gratitude that we have for Lucy for connecting us, for this group, is only exceeded by the humbling gratitude we have for her family's graciousness.

"Everyone, please meet your new neighbor."

The gift here was not a baby, it was the connection that facilitated an adoption, a meaningful connection that came about through generosity and shared stories. The deep gratitude Sylvia and her family feel for this connection had a profound impact on everyone who heard their story, and inspired new desire for connection and personal story-sharing between members of her community.

A NOTE FROM REBECCA, THE LENDING LIBRARIAN

I'm passionate about my personal library of things collection, which takes up a good bit of space in my garage, closets, and drawers. My kids have grown accustomed to hauling boxes of things onto the front porch to lend to neighbors, and I'm especially busy fielding requests for glasses, napkins, silverware, and party supplies from May through September, during the party-graduation-wedding season. Every once in a while, I toy with the idea of passing my collections off to other people to steward, yet each time I'm tempted to retire as a lending librarian, the universe seems to sense this. Inevitably, someone tells me how much they appreciated having glasses to toast at their daughter's wedding or napkins for their church retreat. My favorite comments come from kids whose parents have been borrowing my fabric bunting strands for birthday parties for more than five years now. The last time I loaned them out, the birthday boy said, "Oh, thank you! It's not a party without these hanging up!" This genuine spur-of-the-moment gratitude wasn't a big deal, and the bunting isn't, either, but the quick thanks made me so happy, I came home and made a couple of new strands to add to the collection. Gratitude of the most basic kind, for the use of simple items, can have a profound impact.

We Invite You to Express Gratitude

Start a gratitude journal. This can take any form that you desire— find a beautiful old or gifted notebook, or jot down your thoughts in a Word document on the computer, or use some scrap paper. It doesn't matter what form it takes, this is your space to reflect on the many things you're grateful for.

Gratitude of the most basic kind, for the use of simple items, can have a profound impact.

To start, show yourself some appreciation: take a moment to reflect on what behaviors you've changed since reading this book, and give yourself credit for doing so! Acknowledging the accomplishments you've made and appreciating the work you've done is a great form of self-care. In addition to noting where you've come from in this gratitude journal, remind yourself where you'd like to go. Set some easy goals for what you want to not buy next. Be kind to yourself and find positive words to articulate a new revelation you may have, a work-around to buying that you pledge to carry forth into the future. Put it somewhere where you'll find it when you want to be reminded that curbing our consumerism, sharing more, and buying less feels good. Sharing some of these deeper revelations with your gift economy members can be cathartic, too. Practice gratitude for all that you have—for your community, your home, the food you have. The more you're grateful for what you have and the bounty of gifts that surround you, the easier it is to not buy the things you don't really need.

Now, take five minutes and choose two people that you'd like to thank. Do your thanksgiving in public, if possible. If you have a photo of the item or service they shared with you, share that with your giving group. If not, just post a note or send a group email about why you're grateful, describing just what they did that you're thankful for. If your group is not online, write your thanks down on a piece of paper and place it in the physical space where you all meet, so everyone can see it. And don't forget to think about your friends and loved ones, including the many gifts they bring to your life. We all love to be recognized for the ways we give to those closest to us.

If you practice gratitude every day, in your journal or even in your head before you go to bed, it will bring about enormous health benefits for you, like feeling fewer negative physical symptoms, feeling an increased sense of hope and energy, having a more positive view about your life, and an increase in determination and enthusiasm in general. If studies have proven that gratitude is good for our overall well-being, why not make it a daily practice? We believe that the combination of gratitude and increased giving and receiving in our lives could help you live longer. Harvard's Study of Adult Development set out to study some eight hundred people who were well, who were happy over the course of their lives, from youth to old age. Researchers wanted to know what makes us live happier, healthier, and longer lives. What did they find? Of the six key things they discovered, their sixth revelation was "generativity." Generativity is giving of ourselves, mentoring, guiding, helping, giving gifts, and simply giving back. Become a mentor and guide for other Buy Nothingers in the discussion forum at buynothinggeteverything.com, leading others down this path of healthy sharing and gratitude. You'll be practicing generativity that's good for your longevity and happiness.[2]

JUST THE BEGINNING:
BUY NOTHING FOR LIFE

Now your Buy Nothing journey has come full circle— congratulations on working through the seven-step challenge! You've accomplished so much in a short period of time. Think about the new friends you've made, the natural resources and money you've saved, the space you've cleared, and, of course, the stuff you didn't buy. You've come so far, but this is just the beginning of your Buy Nothing journey. Here are ways to share more and keep it going.

Share Your Experience

Have you been keeping your Buy Nothing challenge a secret? It's time to get the word out. The more friends and family members join you, the more support you'll have as you continue on this path.

It's okay, people might look at you with raised eyebrows when you tell them you're Buying Nothing for a day, a week, or even a month, but most will be intrigued (if even secretly envious) by your new resolve. Talk about it, tell your family about it, ask them to jump on board with you. Tell them why it's important to you— what's your personal motivation for Buying Nothing? If it's to save money, being open with your family about your desire to lower expenses is a great way to motivate reluctant partners and get everyone on board. Or, if you're in this to conserve resources, talk to your family about that, and why you care. If you're all about receiving amazing free gifts, that's okay, too. Tell them what's motivating this change, and they'll understand you a little better and want to join in the experiment.

Once you've done so, invite them to join you. Then they can see for themselves what we're all up to. When we first started on our journey of not buying, we had each other to rely on, but getting our families on board helped keep us motivated and inspired, and made it much easier to stick with our newfound habits.

Start Over and Over and Over Again

We encourage everyone to do the seven steps outlined in this book as a seven-day exercise, and you can continue them in rounds—indefinitely. If you fall off the Buy Nothing wagon, you can start with Step 1 again.

We've designed these exercises as a process of self-discovery and change so that you can work through a system of weaning yourself from buying mindlessly, developing deep self-knowledge, and then blossoming into empowerment and action. This is where inviting others to join you in each step can make this easier and more sustainable, easier to say no to the "shopping date," and suggest coffee or a walk instead. The more you let this lifestyle sink in with those around you, helping them see this isn't a fad diet or even a short-term gimmick but a commitment to changing our behavior en masse, the more they'll want to join you. This is how we can change the world, by bringing one person at a time around to the many joys of Buying Nothing, and the profound effects it can have on us and our planet.

Challenge Yourself to Buy Nothing Longer

Research tells us that people need thirty days to truly change a habit. So, for those of you interested in turning this into a Buy Nothing 30, stick with it. There's a lot packed into each of our steps, whether you do one a day for a week or stretch it out longer. The key will be finding a group of people who are ready to share with you so that you have your immediate support group and gift economy to lean on. Express gratitude there, as often as you can. We promise, it'll be contagious.

In our very first local gift economy on Bainbridge Island, our members regularly shared with one another their gratitude and the lessons they were learning, and the word spread throughout the whole community, bringing new members to the group every day. Just three and a half months after establishing the group, Jill Hendren shared this universal story of gratitude:

"Friday night is usually movie night in our household. It's a nice way to wind down at the end of the week, and my girls (ages seven and nine) look forward to it. Tonight was a bit of a changeup. I was glancing through Buy Nothing when I came upon Alison's post about a six-year-old foster child only coming with the clothes upon her back and no coat. So typical movie night turned into what do we have that she might like . . .

"The girls carefully picked out some things they thought she might like. After gathering all the things, we were going to give them to Alison, but as all you parents know, plans change. So at 8 p.m. I load up the girls and all their gifts, and drive to make their special delivery. The girls were so excited to meet their soon-to-be new friend. I explained she may be in bed, but as luck would have it she was not. :)

"We gave her all her new things. The kids gave her a warm jacket, a variety of clothes, hair accessories, a new toothbrush, a backpack, a few toys. She got the biggest smile on her face and ran up the stairs. A few seconds later she appeared with a little stuffed animal. It was Daisy Duck. She whispered something to her foster mom. Her mom looked at me and said, 'She would like to give this to you.' The little girl leaned forward to give it to me and gave me one of the biggest hugs I ever had. A few minutes later the girls went off to play. I was told later she also tried to give the girls her last and only possession, her bear.

"She had the clothes on her back, two stuffed animals, and she had given me one. This is a priceless lesson on giving freely with no expectations. Thank you, Buy Nothing Bainbridge, I have a new friend, her name is Edith, and she gave me more than just a duck tonight."

Buying Nothing is meant to be an ongoing journey of discovery because, let's face it, you'll be buying and not buying until the day you die. Every time you make a choice to Buy Nothing instead of buying new, you're taking a step in the direction of positive change. Focus on these successes instead of the times you can't Buy Nothing. This is a lifelong journey.

Habits are more easily broken if you can replace them with another behavior. Breaking the habit of driving to a store to get the things you want will be easier when you have a gift economy in place and the behavior of giving, asking, and expressing gratitude under your belt. We realize that because buying things is so ingrained in our everyday culture, it's going to be a tough habit to break, especially in the first couple of weeks, but if you Buy Nothing for a month, and then another month, you will have replaced the urge to shop with the intrigue and inventiveness of sharing. The longer we use these ideas and our own giving networks to replace our automatic impulse to buy, the easier this becomes and the better off we'll all be.

Buy Mindfully

Here's a note about buying, when you do buy. By now, you've likely freed up money, and even some time, from not buying and from borrowing, asking for, and fixing what you already have. So when you do buy, buy used and buy locally as often as possible, to keep objects out of landfills and to support your community and small, local businesses. And buy the best quality item you can. Focus on items that are designed to last, instead of multiple single-use items. Yes, these may cost a bit more, but when you invest in durable items that are not designed to stop functioning in a month or a year or two, you save money, and our landfills, in the long run. There's so much planned obsolescence (products that are meant to not last long, like certain computers and cell phones) in our everyday products that it's worth researching the best items you can buy so that you're putting your hard-earned money toward items that have warranties or excellent reviews or that can be easily fixed. If you buy items made of quality materials, they will last longer.

As you may already know, what and how you buy can be political. To whom do you want to give your money? Which companies and corporations do you value and respect? Be mindful about every purchase by carefully researching the corporations that are taking our money to decide if they deserve our support. Do they have a record of polluting the environment, or do they have fair-trade practices and an end-of-life plan for the products they make? Are they committed to bringing about good in the world? For instance, our two families have found Who Gives a Crap, a company producing recycled, plastic-packaging-free toilet paper with a social conscience. They contribute 50 percent of their profits to the construction of toilets around the world, and we're genuinely happy to spend our money on this special TP each month. Remember that the corporate world is built on consumers, so as a consumer you have the power to vote with your wallet and encourage companies to embrace healthier and more sustainable practices with every purchase you choose to make.

When you are buying, do you buy once? Meaning, do you spend more money on a thing that is so well made, the company so responsible, that they will guarantee it will last as long as you own it? Some manufacturers have this kind of guarantee. Other products, like a classic cast-iron skillet, will simply last forever if you take good care of it. There are a few items, like the cast-iron skillet that we use every day in our kitchens, that we've had for years. For some special products, we may have invested more money in purchasing them because we know that if a flaw shows up, the company will replace it for us and hopefully recycle or fix the broken one so the materials are not wasted. When you *do* finally have to buy items that you use every day, the workhorses of our lives, mindfully researching your options and investing in the best-crafted item can be worth your initial investment.

And remember, a great motto is "First buy at home." There's no better place to shop than your own cupboards and closets. Shop for your next meal in your very own fridge and pantry. It's the cheapest grocery store in town. And, rather than heading out to the mall to buy another outfit, see what you can create from your own closet and drawers. You just may surprise yourself.

When you save money through Buying Nothing, you double your good. You are building a healthier planet and more resilient community, and you can free up some of your cash to invest in the sort of world you want to live in by supporting the people and ideas you believe in.

A VISION FOR THE FUTURE

> ## ANNA'S BUY NOTHING STORY
>
> "A love letter to my fellow Buy-Nothingers. Every time I go to col-
> lect a gifted or borrowed item, I make a point of walking. This
> way I explore new streets and have the time to appreciate them.
> Each time I am met with some previously unknown wonder and
> feel less alien, more unified in our diversity making connections
> I wouldn't have had before. Thank you, group, the generosity and
> joy in gifting and/or using something extraneous to you gives me
> hope that we are becoming more interconnected and intrinsic to
> each other."
>
> —*Anna Debono, Queensland*

Recent research has revealed that trees survive in a forest through
a remarkable network of interconnectedness, each organism tap-
ping into an underground web of fungi to transfer resources to one
another.[1] If we think of ourselves as trees in a forest, we can create a
similar web of connection within our communities, leaning on this
network to meet our needs and support us. When your local collective is strong, you can organize and accomplish so much together.

Now, think of your community as a single tree in an even bigger forest, a forest of giving communities that you can tap into, a broader network of gift economies that are ready and able to be of service to others. These networks within networks can be a powerful tool to bring about good. Once you've learned how to give locally, you can connect globally to accomplish surprising things, all for the greater good. This is our vision for the future, and how Buying Nothing can truly make the world a better place.

Giving Networks as Aid Organizations

Less than a week after the magnitude 7.8 earthquake hit Nepal on April 25, 2015, it became clear that little to no relief had reached villages beyond the capital city of Kathmandu. Roads were dangerous, but even worse, supplies for temporary shelter for the more than two million now homeless had dried up. Tents and tarps were completely sold out in Kathmandu. Foreign governments and aid organizations were stopped at the only international airport in the nation, their incoming relief supplies requisitioned by Nepal customs, so the much-needed food, tents, tarps, blankets, and medical supplies were left sitting on the runway, ultimately for months, tied up in a confounding wad of red tape.

Liesl's friends in Nepal were frantic, texting for any means to get materials to people suffering in remote villages. Family members were still buried underneath the rubble. Aid organizations trucking supplies to villages on the few passable roads were forced to stop en route by groups of people living along the road, desperate for help. There were still tens of thousands of people who had lost everything and were in need of the most basic necessities to survive: food, clean water, sleeping bags, and shelter.

We decided to try something seemingly crazy—to tap into the vast Buy Nothing network to gather supplies and deliver them where needed. The idea was bold and would involve a worldwide network of volunteers, the complicity of some airlines, and some social media hacks. We started in the major cities with thriving local gift economies. Seattle was our first test: Shelley Schwinn, Buy Nothing Project operations manager, posted to some five hundred groups in greater Seattle and through friends who own the Nepali clothing company Sherpa Adventure Gear. We were quickly able to gather, fill, and then send off twenty-two duffels in a private shipping container that Sherpa Adventure Gear put on a flight as part of their regular clothing shipment to Nepal.

Friends in Boulder, Colorado, networked in their climbing community for duffels, tents, tarps, and medical supplies, as did groups in San Francisco, Indiana, Ohio, Massachusetts, New Hampshire, and Washington, DC. We then got word out through our own social networks in all major cities that we were looking for anyone headed to Nepal willing to add a few additional pieces to their luggage. As tourists entering the country, they could whisk right through the airport with their own personal bags filled with tents, tarps, sleeping bags, and medical supplies. We would take care of the airline side of the equation, petitioning excess-baggage departments and receiving waivers from them for humanitarian relief. United Airlines and Etihad were our most supportive airlines, waiving hundreds of bags through their systems as accompanied excess loads headed to the Himalayas with doctors, nurses, climbers, scientists, filmmakers, and volunteers rushing to aid in the relief efforts. Our friends on the ground in Kathmandu— Nepali mountaineers, kayakers, and guides—could then dispatch the supplies and health care up to far-flung villages.

United Airlines pilot Matt Murray volunteered to fly to Nepal for free as a passenger on his days off to single-handedly jet one hundred duffels of tents and tarps into the country. An Everest climber, David Carter, took time off from work in Indiana to fly to Nepal with two of his friends to courier one hundred solar chargers for us. These chargers were instrumental in helping the people of Rasuwa as they rebuilt their village of Langtang, which was completely buried in an avalanche triggered by the earthquake. These individual stories of giving tell a broader narrative of how community-based sharing and gift economy networks can mobilize to make a difference in times of need.

Our Facebook group was mission control, everyone connecting there to circumvent all possible roadblocks. Somehow, we had managed to build secret tunnels to get duffels into Nepal in broad daylight. In the end, in two months' time, the network was able to collect, ship, and deliver two hundred forty duffels filled with more than seven hundred family-size tents and tarps, one hundred solar chargers, blankets, medical supplies, and hundreds of solar lights at little to no cost to us, all before the monsoon arrived. These supplies, valued at more than $67,000, were all provided by everyday people sharing what they had in their attics, garages, and storage rooms. It worked, and showed us what could be possible if we were ever faced with such a disaster again.

We believe this kind of person-to-person worldwide network can make a difference in any disaster and is a viable alternative model that could work in parallel with the larger aid agencies on the ground. Buying Nothing taps into our innate desire to help, and when disaster happens, our giving nature kicks into overdrive. If enough of us take on the seven steps we outline in this book, we'll discover that we can create a powerful local resource and spark the ability to become more resilient and adaptable to anything that might come our way, like power outages, job loss, illness, divorce, wildfires, and hurricanes. The more connected we are, the more we're able to share what we have and provide relief for people in crisis.

If you have a giving group in your hometown, you've taken the first steps in building a resilient community, not only to be able to help individuals within your hometown, but also to be poised and ready to help people farther afield who may just need you one day.

Saving the Earth, One Give, Ask, Share at a Time

We were first inspired to launch the Buy Nothing Project after seeing firsthand the horrible effect plastic has on our environment. It is our hope that as more of us join in this practice of buying less, sharing more, and saying no to plastic, we can reduce our reliance on plastics and halt the devastating environmental damage it creates. Our ultimate goal is to deter plastics from entering our ecosystems to begin with. This starts with us, as consumers. If we refuse to buy plastics, manufacturers will be forced to stop making them.

We can each join this movement and make a lasting individual mark by Buying Nothing every day. Every time we source a shared or used item instead of a new one, we're preventing the depletion of our natural resources. Every time we refuse to buy new, we're avoiding the pollution associated with shipping and trucking those items around the world for purchase. And every time we give or share our once-loved things, we save them from taking up space in expanding landfills. Through every small act of consumer resistance, we can make our own meaningful contributions to curb climate change and environmental pollution.

Real-World Sharing

We started Buy Nothing using a free social media platform to initiate connections that would bring people together in the real world. Our goal is to inspire and enable all of us to share easily in our daily lives, posting our gifts and asks online and offline, wherever we are.

We are currently building an independent platform, Soop.app, to provide the world an online global gift economy hub. Our goal is to build a platform beholden to the public good instead of profit, giving us all access to human-centered digital architecture for a thriving global network of personal gift economies. The design we're working on is informed by everything we've learned leading the Buy Nothing Project, including research that shows there is a limit to the number of people with whom we can maintain stable social relationships and connections. Dr. Robin Dunbar, professor emeritus of evolutionary psychology at the University of Oxford, determined that 150 is the magic, maximum number of individuals each of us can form meaningful relationships with.[2]

We can also initiate our giving outside of social media. Take that first step and ask your local friends to join you once a week or once a month for a sharing get-together. Invite your friends to invite their friends to join you, and so on. You can do it in your home or meet at public parks or a community center. You can meet for fifteen minutes, or an hour or more. You can choose to share specific items each week (clothing, kitchen utensils), or share food, or create a lending library of things.

If communities build gift economies into their infrastructure, giving could happen as part of our daily routine. Canberra, the capital of Australia, has declared itself a "sharing city," creating an interactive map that shows the locations of all of the city's sharing resources and activities, from community gardens and Little Free Libraries, to Buy Nothing Project neighborhood groups.[3] This is a powerful model for all of us to adopt for our own towns and cities.

This Buying Nothing paradigm shift has grown internationally, and scaled quickly, because it's filling a deep need that's been missing in our collective consciousness: the need to share, to connect, to conserve, and to strengthen our resilience through community. This "circular economy," an economy designed to eliminate waste and pollution while keeping materials and items in use, can regenerate and preserve our more natural systems, our communities, our wildlands, and our climate. Together, we can make a difference in the environment, the economy, our own bank accounts, our lives, and the future well-being of our families and neighborhoods.

We hope this book is a blueprint for your household and local community that will bring about positive change beyond our homes, towns, cities, and countries. Our ultimate wish is for this Buy Nothing mind-set to positively impact the world at large. We cannot produce, consume, and landfill our way to a better future given the finite resources on Earth, but we can share our way there. Together, we can change the course of our future—we've already begun.

ACKNOWLEDGMENTS

First and foremost, we want to acknowledge the millions of people around the world, including everyone in Samdzong, Upper Mustang, Nepal participating in local gift economies and pursuing Buy Nothing actions of their own to steward materials wisely, share resources, and care for one another and our planet. This diversity of individual action adds up to collective positive impact and systemic change, and we are deeply grateful to everyone who has come before us on this path, to those we walk with now, and to everyone who will join in.

The Buy Nothing Project would be just one group on one little island if not for the dedication and passion of our founding team, including Shelley Schwinn, our favorite kraken; Crescent Moegling, our favorite mapping wizard who also helped with research and releases for this book; John Brownlow, who asks the tough questions and then steps in to help and produce the most professionally perfect assets one might need for a project at any moment; everyone in the original Buy Nothing Bainbridge groups who willingly acts as guinea pig for beta testing of each new idea; the entire Buy Nothing Project Global Team, including Cheryl Baker, Jennifer Rockenbaugh, Eileen Edwards, Michelle Edwards, Alexa Carey, Ann Gerrietts, Rachel Anderson, Antoinette Sankar, Daria Kelsey, Katherine Parsons, Marlene Schulz, Kristina M. Ione, Emma Jag,

Kate Watkins, Laura Norris, Robynn Coulter, Kym Ianetta, Francine Levesque, Adrienne O'Reilly-Angus, Rora Melendy, Lissa Jagodnik, and Lillian Lu; all Regional Team volunteers and Local Admin volunteers—our beloved "vollies," as our friends in Australia have taught us to call them—and all group members, everywhere. We are also grateful to everyone who contributed their stories and perspectives to be shared in this book.

Liesl would like to give thanks to her mom, Gretel, for being her lifelong role model, from feminism to gardening to love of the outdoors to beekeeping. Gretel's spearheading of the first weekly curbside composting program east of Michigan has inspired Liesl to do her own community activism. Liesl's dad's can-do optimism has instilled the deep sense that absolutely everything in life is possible, even going where no humans have trod before. To her children, Finn and Cleo, she offers her purest and humblest thanks for forbearing a childhood of exploration and experimentation lived different from other children. As Grandma and most mothers famously say, "You'll thank me later." And to Liesl's husband, Pete Athans, no words could possibly speak to the depths of her love, awe, and gratitude for Pete's grace and formidable energy, always taking care of everyone around him. Liesl's special deep gratitude also goes to her siblings, Bryn, Heidi, and Joc, and their incredibly supportive spouses and children for providing the joy, passion, laughter, competitiveness, trials, tribulations, compassion, and adventure a lifetime of family love can sustain. To Ang Temba and Yangin Sherpa, Liesl's family soul mates, *"thujeche"* for the life lessons you have taught us. We miss you every single day and wish we could live closer together in the same loving community.

Rebecca would like to give special thanks to her mother, Anita

Frankel Rockefeller, and father, Phil Rockefeller, whose unflagging dedication to public service, feminism, and environmental and social justice has provided a clear and compelling life's work map. Gratitude for lived examples, conversations, stories, guidance, education, food, cups of tea, great ideas, and assistance with roadside emergencies and existential crises to everyone who makes her life as a working single parent possible and meaningful, including Inge Frankel, ל″ז; Nat Frankel, ל″ז; Aileen Frankel; Nancy Zises; Barry Frankel; Melissa Rockefeller; Minh, Peter, and Lilou Pham; Airyka Rockefeller; Larry Weiner; Jillian Worth; Kasper Luna; Nina Runstein Minney; Liza Pascal; Ayan Rivera; Jenn Gallucci; Mino and Lexia Christante; Michele Lang; the entire Gazzam Lake coven; Naomi Spinak; Zann Jacobrown; Julie Rosenblatt; Kay McGowan and the entire IWC team; Deb Buitenveld; Jenny Mayfield; Maria Knighton; M'Rissa C; everyone at ITA; Understanding; Strong and Magic Israel; Lori Levari; Jamie Rudman Kloosterman; Jill Franklin; Melinda Gordon Blum; Sheri Lynn; and all the JBs. Her deepest gratitude and respect to Ava and Mira for adding so much thought, elbow grease, patience, and humor to the shared work of repairing the world.

Our heartfelt gratitude to our literary agent, Neeti Madan of Sterling Lord Literistic, who reached out to us two years ago with the vision that we just might have a book in us to write. Thank you for believing in us and lighting the way through the inner world of bookmaking. We are also deeply inspired by the guidance given to us by our editor, Sarah Pelz of Atria/Simon & Schuster, who has shaped our narrative in a gentle, clear, and supportive way. We knew you were the perfect editor for us when you told us you were a member of your own local Buy Nothing group. We're also ever grateful for the behind-the-scenes contributions of Melanie Iglesias Perez at Atria and the entire Atria team. Angelina Krahn's copyediting has kept us on our toes, down to every last fact. Thanks also to Jason Chappell for his guidance during the copyediting process. And to Brooke Budner, a deep bow to you for your beautiful illustrations.

APPENDIX

Rethink Your Trash

We're taking that trash-to-treasure motto literally here—don't laugh. Did you know that your trash tells you a lot about yourself and your buying habits? When you consume less, you generate less waste. And inventorying your trash will also help you better understand the ways you can reduce your waste, or give it away for someone else to use creatively. Not only is this environmentally healthier, but you'll save money on your weekly trash pickup or save time from dropping off trash less frequently.

It's easy and convenient to not think too hard about what happens to your trash once it's hauled away, but *away* is typically a landfill or an incinerator. We've reduced each of our own families' trash enough that we've opted out of the weekly trash and yard-waste pickup that costs a Seattle family a minimum of $247 a year.[1] We fill our thirty-two-gallon can every three to four months. Really! When it's full, we take it to the local transfer station. Our total cost for dumping trash is ten dollars per trash can. That's a yearly savings of almost $200. Not bad.

The great benefit of inventorying your trash is that doing so highlights obvious waste streams that you can possibly share with others (one woman's trash is another woman's treasure), Recycle, or Reuse elsewhere. You may even find things in your trash that'll help you Buy Nothing.

Some people feel understandably squeamish about touching garbage. But what makes trash yucky once you throw it away? It wasn't yucky when you were holding it in your hand before putting it in your garbage can. If you remove the organic waste from your trash (and compost it instead, see page 237), then your waste should only be dry goods, all just as clean as they were when you tossed 'em in your bin. If you throw away anything sharp like broken glass or needles, please always be sure to put them in a container so no one will get hurt by the sharp objects.

Okay, that said, let's get started. Pull out that garbage can and start lifting items out of it. Here's what you're looking for:

RECYCLABLES

Go online and figure out what belongs in the recycle bin. Look up your city or town's waste management site by searching "[Name of your town] + recycling." Make a copy of the list and familiarize yourself with it. Stick it on your recycle bin if that helps (we do, it changes regularly). What kinds of plastics can be recycled? Usually they'll tell you precisely which items are acceptable. While it's tempting to throw in every plastic item, it's important to follow the list exactly; items that don't belong will contaminate an entire batch and send everything to the landfill. What other recyclables can be put in your municipal recycling bin? Paper? Glass? Aluminum cans? Milk cartons? Pull all those items out of your trash and place them in your recycling. What's left over? Plastics you can't recycle? Would you consider not buying that item, or buying an alternative that comes without the nonrecyclable plastic? Or can you stockpile that plastic item and find someone who could use it, like art teachers, upcyclers, or canners? Our local recycling program won't accept Tetra Paks (a carton for juices and soups, for example, made of layers of paperboard, plastic, and aluminum), and there are a couple of items made of Tetra Paks that we have a tough time living without. We stockpile our empty Tetra Paks and hand them off to a friend who puts them in her curbside recycling in nearby Seattle. That's one work-around. Styrofoam meat trays are always appreciated by our local art programs (more about this on page 185).

PAPER

When it comes to recycling paper, recyclers typically take all paper, not just newspapers and printer paper. Cardboard boxes usually have to be separated out, broken down, and placed on the curb. Be sure to also include paperboard like cereal boxes in your paper recycling, unless you know of an art studio that would like to use it. There are other hidden papers, too, like your toilet paper rolls, and the paperboard that backs things like batteries and lightbulbs. Put *all* paper in your recycling, even if it means you're standing beside your trash bin ripping at things to separate the plastic parts from the paper. It can get physical, but it feels good, partly because it's one less thing you're paying to throw away, one less thing to populate the landfill, and one more thing you're adding to the recycle bin.

Even better, stave off paper in the first place. One way is to reduce the amount of junk mail you get. In the US, Catalog Choice is a great website and app for stopping unwanted junk mail in its tracks. Calling up the companies that send you mail is always an option, too, and apps like PaperKarma are easy to use and a great way to let companies know you don't want their paper waste coming to your door.

GARBOLOGY

Surprisingly, paper is still taking up the lion's share of room in our landfills. When archaeologists who called themselves "garbologists" started doing the first proper "digs" in landfills in the 1990s, they made a remarkable discovery. The assumption was that plastics would be, by volume, one of the biggest culprits occupying our landfills. But surprisingly, it wasn't. Manufacturers had successfully made plastic bottles and bags thinner, so they were not taking up as much room as some of the other common household materials. It was paper that took up the most room. This revelation was eye-opening, because the assumption was that paper would decompose since it's made of organic material. It didn't.

The late Dr. William Rathje, the Garbage Project's lead scientist, noted that paper, some thirty feet down in a landfill, was still perfectly intact, having been entombed deep in the garbage with no light, water, or air to break it down. Paper, they found, was taking up nearly 50 percent of the space in our landfills.[2] Today, it occupies about 25 percent, but it's still the single most populous material in landfills.[3] Surely we can make a dent in that by recycling it, even if it means we're ripping out and salvaging the paper from the thermoformed blister pack plastics around our toothbrushes and Hot Wheels toys.

POLYETHYLENE

Polyethylene is just a fancy name for the material used for plastic bags, or film. Most supermarkets will take your clean and dry polyethylene, so you should be keeping it out of your landfill trash. This includes produce bags, newspaper bags, zip top food storage bags (wash 'em out, see how to make your own bag dryer on page 98), product wrap for paper towels and bathroom tissue, electronic device wrap, cereal box liners, bread bags, and dry cleaning bags. You'll be surprised how much of your waste is polyethylene.

Your landfill trash should be looking pretty slim now.

FOOD AND ORGANIC MATERIAL

Food waste is, by weight, the biggest yearly contributor to land-fills.[4] So waste management companies use up a lot of fossil fuels to cart your food waste to the landfill, where it'll rot and emit methane into the atmosphere. And yet we know it's a resource that someone near you could really use. If you don't have a compost bin or worm bin, chickens, or a dog, save those food scraps in a bucket and give them away in your local gift economy. Rebecca has given up on her home compost bin (on account of very tenacious wild rats), but her daughter's guinea pig eats almost everything her hens don't like. Don't be shy, just let it be known that you have food and vegetable scraps available every few days for composting, or for feeding chickens, rabbits, guinea pigs, etc., and you'll find takers. The more scraps they feed their animals, the less store-bought food they have to buy. And, as soon as you take the food out of your trash, you'll see a major reduction in your daily output of waste (and your trash will smell much better, too!). If this feels extreme to you, check your municipal waste service. Many cities now offer compost pickup along with recycling and landfill waste. And you can always start your own compost bin to turn your waste into "black gold" for houseplants, windowsill herbs, and roof gardens.

There may be some more things still sitting in your trash that you could toss into the compost bin. You might be surprised at what we put in ours. Here's a short list we've compiled over the years.

What We Compost: pet fur, baskets, wine at the bottom of the glass, sugar packets, shredded paper, ashes from the fireplace and firepit, paper produce stickers, butter wrappers (these really do break down), wax paper (but it also makes great fire starter), cotton string, baling twine, balloons (the latex kind only), cornstarch packing peanuts, crushed eggshells (the worms love 'em), cotton swabs (the kind with the paper applicators, nonplastic), nutshells (they do break down, but can also go in the fire starter), fruit pits (we get sprouted peach trees each year), sheep's wool (we have lots for crafting), kombucha SCOBY (hens love it, but it can go in the compost, too), half-burned matchsticks, old seeds and their packets (we might get some freebie veggies the next season), pencil shavings from the sharpener, paper lollipop sticks, wax-coated-paper candy wrappers, masking tape, parchment paper, old potpourri, old baking soda, nontoxic playdough, latex rubber bands, corn husks and cobs, paper towels and tissues, plastic-free tea bags and paper wrappers, paper scraps, old herbs and spices, entire fish (these get buried way down in the pile), and avocado pits (the worms love the decomposing avocado pits and lay their eggs in them, think worm nursery).

For us, our veggie scrap waste is at least two-thirds of our overall waste. And it all gets used up. And, don't forget, if you keep a big jar in your fridge or freezer to hold your vegetable scraps like onion and garlic skins, it makes the perfect base for vegetable broth. You'll never have to buy veggie broth again.

So what's left in your trash bin? Not so much, right? By refamiliarizing ourselves with our recyclables list, pulling all plastic bags out of our trash, and rethinking what can be composted or fed to animals, we're left with a few random items . . . and of course we have a Buy Nothing plan for those. Bear with us here, there's a method to this madness. We save the following to be recycled in special places or given away to someone who needs them:

- **Metal items, batteries, and e-waste** (connectors, cords, broken hard drives)—These can be recycled at special places. In our hometown, we can take these items to our transfer station, where there are bins for them. Some cities and towns have special drop-off days for these waste streams. Search online for this recycling information by typing in your city's name, "recycling information about," and the name of the item you want to dispose of.
- **Tetra Paks**—We save these for disposal in Seattle in our friends' recycle bins since we can't recycle them at home.
- **Wine corks, metal bottle caps, padded mailers, bubble wrap, textiles, and Styrofoam meat trays**—If you can't Reuse these common waste items at home, offer them to someone else. They can be used for shipping, art, and classroom projects.

Think creatively the next time you go to toss something—and offer it in your giving network instead. You never know who might need it! If we can get comfortable having a dialogue about what's in our waste, throw away less, feel no shame about it, and share more, we know we can help reduce carbon emissions, rethink consumption, and spark creative Reuse around the world.

REFERENCES

Why We Should Buy Nothing

1 "What Are Microplastics?," Ocean Facts, National Oceanic and Atmospheric Administration, updated June 25, 2018, oceanservice.noaa.gov/facts/micro plastics.html.

2 When Plastic Outnumbers Plankton: Insights into the Great Pacific Garbage Patch, U.S. Mission to ASEAN, accessed May 12, 2017, https://asean.usmis sion.gov/innovasean_20150615/.

3 "Marine Debris Is Everyone's Problem," poster, Woods Hole Sea Grant, https://www.whoi.edu/fileserver.do?id=107364&pt=2&p=88817.

4 US Environmental Protection Agency, *State of the Science White Paper: Effects of Plastics Pollution on Aquatic Life and Aquatic-Dependent Wildlife*, December 2016, https://www.epa.gov/sites/production/files/2017-02/documents /tfw-trash_free_waters_plastics-aquatic-life-report-2016-12.pdf.

5 World Economic Forum, *The New Plastics Economy: Rethinking the Future of Plastics*, January 2016, www3.weforum.org/docs/WEF_The_New_Plastics _Economy.pdf.

6 Fabiano Barretto, "Citizen Science Summit on Plastics Pollution in the Salish Sea," Global Garbage, March 30, 2010, http://www.globalgarbage.org/blog /index.php/2010/03/30/citizen-science-summit-on-plastics-pollution-in -the-salish-sea/.

7 North Sea Foundation, Marine Conservation Society, Seas at Risk, and Plastic Soup Foundation, *Micro Plastics in Personal Care Products*, position paper, August 2012, www.mcsuk.org/downloads/pollution/positionpaper-micro plastics-august2012.pdf; Plastic Soup Foundation, "Beat the Microbead," updated August 20, 2019.

8 Simon Reddy, "Plastic Pollution Affects Sea Life Throughout the Ocean," Pew Charitable Trusts, September 24, 2018, https://www.pewtrusts.org/en /research-and-analysis/articles/2018/09/24/plastic-pollution-affects-sea -life-throughout-the-ocean.

9 "Facts and Figures on Marine Pollution," Unesco, accessed September 27, 2019, http://www.unesco.org/new/en/natural-sciences/ioc-oceans/focus-areas

/rio-20-ocean/blueprint-for-the-future-we-want/marine-pollution/facts-and
-figures-on-marine-pollution/.

10 "Toxicological Threats of Plastic," EPA, accessed June 19, 2017, www.epa.gov
/trash-free-waters/toxicological-threats-plastic.

11 Madeleine Smith, David C. Love, Chelsea M. Rochman, and Roni A. Neff, "Microplastics in Seafood and the Implications for Human Health," *Current Environmental Health Reports* 5, no. 3 (2018): 375–86, doi:10.1007/s40572-018-0206-z.

12 Sarah Knapton, "Plastic Weighing Equivalent of One Billion Elephants Has
Been Made since 1950s and Most Is Now Landfill," *Telegraph*, July 19, 2017,
www.telegraph.co.uk/science/2017/07/19/plastic-weighing-equivalent-one
-billion-elephants-has-made-since/.

13 Diana Ivanova, Konstantin Stadler, Kjartan Steen-Olsen, Richard Wood, Gi-
bran Vita, Arnold Tukker, and Edgar G. Hertwich, "Environmental Impact As-
sessment of Household Consumption," *Journal of Industrial Ecology* 20, no. 3
(2016): doi: 10.1111/jiec.12371.

14 "CO2 Emissions (Metric Tons Per Capita)," World Bank, https://data.world
bank.org/indicator/EN.ATM.CO2E.PC.

15 "Greenhouse Gas Equivalencies Calculator," EPA, updated December 2018,
www.epa.gov/energy/greenhouse-gas-equivalencies-calculator.

16 "Summary for Policymakers of IPCC Special Report on Global Warming of 1.5°C
Approved by Governments," Intergovernmental Panel on Climate Change, October 8, 2018, www.ipcc.ch/2018/10/08/summary-for-policymakers-of-ipcc
-special-report-on-global-warming-of-1-5c-approved-by-governments/.

17 Christian Jarrett, "The Psychology of Stuff and Things," *Psychologist* 26, no. 8
(August 2013): 560–4, thepsychologist.bps.org.uk/volume-26/edition-8/psy
chology-stuff-and-things.

18 Alana Semuels, "We Are All Accumulating Mountains of Things," *Atlantic*,
August 21, 2018, https://www.theatlantic.com/technology/archive/2018/08
/online-shopping-and-accumulation-of-junk/567985/.

19 Jeanne E. Arnold, *Life at Home in the Twenty-First Century: 32 Families Open
Their Doors*, (Los Angeles: Cotsen Institute of Archaeology Press, 2017).

20 *A Cluttered Life: Middle-Class Abundance*, episode 1, "Stuff," UCTV video, 6:33,
posted December 23, 2013, www.uctv.tv/shows/Stuff-A-Cluttered-Life-Mid
dle-Class-Abundance-Ep-1-24699.

21 "Object Ethnography Project," Max Liboiron, accessed December 2018,
https://maxliboiron.com/2013/08/07/object-ethnography-project/.

22 "A Conversation with Tim Kasser," *The True Cost* (blog), accessed January 7,
2016, https://truecostmovie.com/tim-kasser-interview/index.html.

Step 1: Give

1 Choongwon Jeong, Andrew T. Ozga, David B. Witonsky, Helena Malmström,
Hanna Edlund, Courtney A. Hofman, Richard W. Hagan, Mattias Jakobsson,
Cecil M. Lewis, Mark S. Aldenderfer, Anna Di Rienzo, and Christina Warinner,

"Long-Term Genetic Stability and a High-Altitude East Asian Origin for the Peoples of the High Valleys of the Himalayan Arc," *PNAS* 113, no. 27 (2016): 7485–90, doi:10.1073/pnas.1520844113.

2 Marie Kondo, *The Life-Changing Magic of Tidying Up: The Japanese Art of Decluttering and Organizing* (Berkeley: Ten Speed Press, 2014).

3 Margareta Magnusson, *The Gentle Art of Swedish Death Cleaning: How to Free Yourself and Your Family from a Lifetime of Clutter* (New York: Scribner, 2018).

4 Genevieve Vaughan, ed., *Women and the Gift Economy: A Radically Different Worldview Is Possible* (Toronto: Inanna Publications and Education, 2007).

5 Mitch Lipka, "Are Women More Generous Than Men?" *Money*, December 1, 2015, money.com/money/4130729/women-more-generous-than-men/.

6 "Study: Poor Are More Charitable Than the Wealthy," *All Things Considered*, NPR, August 8, 2010, www.npr.org/templates/story/story.php?storyId=129068241.

7 Tanya Misseghers, "Buy Nothing Group Connects Local Residents," *Winnipeg Free Press*, March 11, 2019, www.winnipegfreepress.com/our-communities/lance/correspondent/Buy-Nothing-group-connects-local-residents-506997071.html.

Step 2: Ask

1 Charles Eisenstein, "The Longing for Belonging," *HuffPost*, updated August 19, 2016, www.huffpost.com/entry/indigeneity-and-belonging_b_8011302.

2 Charles Eisenstein, *Sacred Economics: Money, Gift & Society in the Age of Transition* (Berkeley: North Atlantic Books, 2011).

3 Linda Babcock and Sara Laschever, *Women Don't Ask: The High Cost of Avoiding Negotiation—and Positive Strategies for Change* (Princeton, NJ: Princeton University Press, 2013).

4 Eisenstein, *Sacred Economics*.

5 Alexandre Tanzi, "U.S. Credit Card Debt Closed 2018 at a Record $870 Billion," *Bloomberg*, March 5, 2019, www.bloomberg.com/news/articles/2019-03-05/u-s-credit-card-debt-closed-2018-at-a-record-870-billion.

6 Elisa Jaffe, "Strangers Come Together to Organize Couple's Dream Wedding," KOMONews, November 19, 2014, https://komonews.com/news/local/strangers-come-together-to-organize-couples-dream-wedding.

7 Scott Greenstone, "Buy Nothing Project: Free Clothes, Toys, Food—Even a Wedding," *Seattle Times*, updated September 29, 2017, www.seattletimes.com/business/local-business/buy-nothing-project-free-clothes-toys-food-even-a-wedding/.

Step 3: Reuse & Refuse

1 "Recycling Means Business," Institute for Local Self-Reliance, February 1, 2002, https://ilsr.org/recycling-means-business/.

2 "Textiles: Material-Specific Data," EPA, accessed May 7, 2019, https://www.epa.gov/facts-and-figures-about-materials-waste-and-recycling/textiles-material-specific-data.

3 "FAQ's," US Food Waste Challenge, Office of the Chief Economist, USDA, https://www.usda.gov/oce/foodwaste/faqs.htm.

4 J. Rovenský et al., "Eggshell Calcium in the Prevention and Treatment of Osteoporosis," *International Journal of Pharmacological Research*, 23 no. 2–3 (2003): 83–92, https://www.ncbi.nlm.nih.gov/pubmed/15018022.

5 Vanesa Benítez, Esperanza Mollá, María A. Martín-Cabrejas, Yolanda Aguilera, Francisco J. López-Andréu, Katherine Cools, Leon A. Terry, and Rosa M. Esteban, "Characterization of Industrial Onion Wastes (Allium cepa L.): Dietary Fibre and Bioactive Compounds," *Plant Foods for Human Nutrition* 66, no. 1 (2011): 48–57, doi: 10.1007/s11130-011-0212-x.

6 Mark Bittman, "Simplest Roast Chicken Recipe," Cooking, *New York Times*, September 8, 2011, https://cooking.nytimes.com/recipes/1015812-simplest -roast-chicken.

7 Katherine Martinko, "How to Avoid Using Paper Towels," TreeHugger, January 8, 2018, www.treehugger.com/cleaning-organizing/how-avoid-using-pa per-towels.html.

8 Ocean Conservancy and International Coastal Cleanup, *Building a Clean Swell: 2018 Report* (Washington, DC: Ocean Conservancy, 2018), oceancon servancy.org/wp-content/uploads/2018/07/Building-A-Clean-Swell.pdf.

9 "Fact Sheet: Single Use Plastics," Earth Day Network, March 29, 2018, www .earthday.org/2018/03/29/fact-sheet-single-use-plastics/.

10 P. Wesley Schultz and Steven R. Stein, "Executive Summary: Litter in America —2009 National Litter Research Findings and Recommendations," Keep America Beautiful, 2009, https://www.kab.org/sites/default/files/News%26Info _Research_LitterinAmerica_ExecutiveSummary_Final.pdf.

11 "EWG's Bottled Water Scorecard, 2011: How Much Do We Drink?" Environmental Working Group, January 25, 2012, www.ewg.org/research/ewg-bot tled-water-scorecard-2011/how-much-do-we-drink.

12 Katie Langin, "Millions of Americans Drink Potentially Unsafe Tap Water. How Does Your County Stack Up?" *Science*, February 12, 2018, https://www .sciencemag.org/news/2018/02/millions-americans-drink-potentially-un safe-tap-water-how-does-your-county-stack.

13 Deborah Blum, "A Threat to Male Fertility," *Well* (blog), *New York Times*, March 21, 2014, well.blogs.nytimes.com/2014/03/21/a-threat-to-male-fertility/.

14 Tim Harford, "How Plastic Became a Victim of Its Own Success," BBC News, September 25, 2017, www.bbc.com/news/business-41188462.

15 Lauren Levy, "The Best Reusable Straw Is Made of Silicone and Burns Into Biodegradable Ash," The Strategist, *New York* magazine, July 12, 2018, http:// nymag.com/strategist/article/best-reusable-straws.html.

16 C. Stevenson, "Plastic Debris in the California Marine Ecosystem: A Summary of Current Research, Solution Strategies and Data Gaps," University of Southern California Sea Grant, Synthetic Report, California Ocean Science Trust (Oakland: University of Southern California Sea Grant, 2011).

17 Susan Freinkel, *Plastic: A Toxic Love Story* (New York: Houghton Mifflin Harcourt, 2011).

18 Mark Anthony Browne, Phillip Crump, Stewart J. Niven, Emma Teuten, Andrew Tonkin, Tamara Galloway, and Richard Thompson, "Accumulation of Microplastic on Shorelines Worldwide: Sources and Sinks," *Environmental Science & Technology* 45, no. 21 (2011): 9175–79, doi: 10.1021/es201811s.

19 Kara Lavender Law, "Plastics in the Marine Environment," *Annual Review of Marine Science* 9, no. 1 (2017): 205–29, doi:10.1146/annurev-marine-010816-060409.

Step 4: Reflect

1 Alana Semuels, "'We Are All Accumulating Mountains of Things,'" *Atlantic*, August 21, 2018, www.theatlantic.com/technology/archive/2018/08/online-shopping-and-accumulation-of-junk/567985/.

2 Hattie Crisell, "Do You Spend £1042 on Clothes Each Year? New Research Reveals the Average Brit's Shopping Habits," *Telegraph*, March 23, 2017, www.telegraph.co.uk/fashion/news/do-spend-1042-clothes-year-new-research-reveals-average-brits/.

Step 5: Make & Fix

1 Isabel V. Sawhill and Christopher Pulliam, "Six Facts About Wealth in the United States," *Brookings*, June 25, 2019, https://www.brookings.edu/blog/up-front/2019/06/25/six-facts-about-wealth-in-the-united-states/.

2 Jeff Weiner, "What's Your Dream Job?," survey results, SurveyMonkey, www.surveymonkey.com/mp/jeff-weiner-survey-results/.

3 Pagan Kennedy, "How to Get High on Soil," *Atlantic*, January 31, 2012, www.theatlantic.com/health/archive/2012/01/how-to-get-high-on-soil/251935/; C. A. Lowry, J. H. Hollis, A. de Vries, B. Pan, L. R. Brunet, J. R. F. Hunt, J. F. R. Paton, E. van Kampen, D. M. Knight, A. K. Evans, G. A. W. Rook, and S. L. Lightman, "Identification of an Immune-Responsive Mesolimbocortical Serotonergic System: Potential Role in Regulation of Emotional Behavior," *Neuroscience* 146, no. 2 (2007): 756–72, doi:10.1016/j.neuroscience.2007.01.067.

4 Janet Raloff, "BPA Found Beached and at Sea," *Science News*, updated September 23, 2013, www.sciencenews.org/blog/science-public/bpa-found-beached-and-sea.

5 Britta Fängström, Anna Strid, Philippe Grandjean, Pál Weihe, and Åke Bergman, "A Retrospective Study of PBDEs and PCBs in Human Milk from the Faroe Islands," *Environmental Health* 4, no. 1 (2005): doi:10.1186/1476-069x-4-12.

6 Jennifer Grayson, "Flowers May Be Nice for Mom, but They're Terrible for Mother Earth," *Washington Post*, May 7, 2015, www.washingtonpost.com/opinions/flowers-may-be-nice-for-mom-but-theyre-terrible-for-mother-earth/2015/05/07/fb69f9f4-f4d5-11e4-b2f3-af5479e6bbdd_story.html.

Step 6: Share, Lend & Borrow

1 Lisa Deaderick, "Building a Community, Ocean Beach-Style," *San Diego Union-Tribune*, January 14, 2017, www.sandiegouniontribune.com/lifestyle/people/sd-me-one-mcateer-20170112-story.html.

2 Isaac Olson, "'It Is Actually Free': Montreal Man Gives Away Heaps of Farm-Fresh Veggies Every Week," CBC News, October 21, 2018, www.cbc.ca/news/canada/montreal/montreal-man-offers-free-vegetables-to-create-sharing-culture-1.4868236.

Step 7: Gratitude

1 "Giving Thanks Can Make You Happier," *Healthbeat*, Harvard Health Publishing, Harvard Medical School, www.health.harvard.edu/healthbeat/giving-thanks-can-make-you-happier.

2 George E. Vaillant, *Aging Well: Surprising Guideposts to a Happier Life from the Landmark Harvard Study of Adult Development* (New York: Little, Brown, 2003).

A Vision for the Future

1 Monika A. Gorzelak, Amanda K. Asay, Brian J. Pickles, and Suzanne W. Simard, "Inter-Plant Communication through Mycorrhizal Networks Mediates Complex Adaptive Behaviour in Plant Communities," *AoB PLANTS* 7 (2015): plv050, https://doi.org/10.1093/aobpla/plv050.

2 Maria Konnikova, "The Limits of Friendship," *New Yorker*, June 20, 2017, www.newyorker.com/science/maria-konnikova/social-media-affect-math-dunbar-number-friendships.

3 Blake Foden, "'A Beautiful Concept': Canberra's Shared Resources Mapped Out," *Canberra Times*, October 21, 2018, www.canberratimes.com.au/story/6001541/a-beautiful-concept-canberras-shared-resources-mapped-out/.

Appendix

1 "Factbox: What America's Largest Cities Charge for Residential Garbage Pick-Up," Reuters, September 21, 2015, https://www.reuters.com/article/us-usa-chicago-garbage-factbox/factbox-what-americas-largest-cities-charge-for-residential-garbage-pick-up-idUSKCN0RM00K20150922.

2 Lauren Ina, "American Journal," *Washington Post*, July 6, 1990, www.washingtonpost.com/archive/politics/1990/07/06/american-journal/00098586-7ec8-4dcf-be76-d4970b8ef91c/.

3 "Paper and Paperboard: Material-Specific Data," EPA, accessed August 6, 2019, www.epa.gov/facts-and-figures-about-materials-waste-and-recycling/paper-and-paperboard-material-specific-data.

4 "FAQ's," USDA.

INDEX

flowerpots, plastic, 188

flowers, 186

folding tables and chairs, 204

food, 93, 94, 123, 190
  composting of, 153–54,
    234, 238
  foraging for, 94–95
  reusing of, 90–95

food waste, 90–91, 237–39

foraging, 94–95

fossil fuels, 142

Freecycle, 188

freezer bags, 98

Freinkel, Susan, 112

friends, interdependence with,
  27

friends network, 46, 68, 79, 131,
  133, 179, 224, 227

fruit vinegar, 149–50

Furness, Storm, 83–84

furniture, 39, 58, 89, 112, 117, 127

future, 43, 106, 213
  Buy Nothing vision for,
    222–28
  shareocracy of, 172–73

G

games, 186

garbage bags, 97

Garbage Project, 236

garden gloves, 174–75, 183

gardens:
  community, 152, 228
  sharing of, 177, 190
  sharing produce from,
    181–82

garden tools and machines, 201

garlic, 94

garlic presses, 121

gemachim, 35

Generation Z, 87

generativity, 214

generosity, 10, 40, 51

*Gentle Art of Swedish Death Clean-
ing, The* (Magnusson), 46

Gen Xers, 143

Georgia, University of, 16

gift economies, 25, 26, 132, 146
  core assumptions of, 61
  creating of, 52–55
  equal value of gifts in,
    72–75
  gratitude in, 72, 208–9,
    213, 217
  indigenous, 23
  interpersonal connected-
    ness in, 40, 62–63, 72,
    131, 133
  lending in, 173; *see also*
    lending
  local, 6, 9, 20, 38, 50, 70,
    127, 217

ABOUT THE AUTHORS

Writer, director, and cinematographer Liesl Clark has produced more than twenty one-hour documentaries on science and exploration for *NOVA*, National Geographic, and the BBC. She has won numerous awards for her journalistic work, including a Primetime Emmy, the Silver Dragon, the Silver Hugo, and the duPont-Columbia Journalism Award: the Gold Baton. As director of the Magic Yeti Children's Libraries, Liesl is working to increase literacy for children in six remote villages in Nepal. She; her husband, Pete Athans; and their two teens, Finn and Cleo, love to explore and live in the highest places where humans can thrive. *The Buy Nothing, Get Everything Plan* is her first book.

• • •

Always on a mission, social media and storytelling coach Rebecca Rockefeller has been working to build a more resilient and equitable world through the Buy Nothing Project, a worldwide network of hyperlocal gift economies. A graduate of the Evergreen State College, Rebecca has spent time as a teacher, community organizer, nonprofit executive director, and writer. She has been most transformed and inspired by her work raising her two kind and wise daughters, Ava Justice and Mira Shalom. Together, they raise chickens, farm food, and grow flowers on an island in the Salish Sea. *The Buy Nothing, Get Everything Plan* is her first book.